CHOOSING THE PRESIDENT

1980 Edition

Published For
The League of Women Voters
Education Fund

Thomas Nelson Publishers
Nashville

ACKNOWLEDGMENTS

To give due credit to the labors of others in the making of a book is always a difficult task. This is more than ordinarily the case with *Choosing The President,* which has been appearing for some time in editions tied to presidential election years. This edition builds on the 1972 version (principally the work of Mary Morgan, with the help of Daphne White) and on the 1976 edition. The latter reflected significant changes in campaign finance law, in the parties' nominating processes, in the presidency itself, and in people's perceptions of it. The research and major revisions necessitated by these changes were done by Annette Kornblum, under the supervision of Beth Perkins, with rewriting and editing by Madelyn A. Bonsignore. Of special help in preparing the 1976 edition were interviews with Ralph Murphine of Matt Reese & Associates, Joseph Gorman of the Congressional Research Service, Michael Malbin of the *National Journal,* and Arthur T. Hadley, author.

The revisions for this edition, which has been updated to help citizens understand and participate in the 1980 presidential election process, were made by League of Women Voters Education Fund staff member Sheri Lanoff, with the help of Karen Lebovich. They wish to acknowledge with particular gratitude the help of Carol Casey of the Congressional Research Service, who provided information for the delegate selection chart in both the 1976 and this 1980 edition.

CONTENTS

Acknowledgments   3

1. On choosing the president   7
2. The political framework: The parties   10
   The role of parties   10
   Party structure   12
   Other political groups   15
   A closer look at third parties   16

3. The political framework: The voters   18
   The expansion of the suffrage   18
   Voter turnout and procedural problems   19
   Voter behavior   22

4. Phase one: The preliminaries   24
   In-party preliminaries   24
   Out-party preliminaries   26
   The media in the preliminaries   28

5. Phase two: Delegate selection—the convention game
   begins   30
   Methods of choosing delegates   30
   Critiques of the primary system   33
   Delegate selection by state (chart)   34
   Democratic party reform   37
   Republican party reform   38

6. Phase three: The national nominating conventions   39
   The functions of national conventions   39
   The gathering of the delegates   41
   Convention makeup   42
   Committee work   44
   Nominating the president   48
   Choosing the vice-president   50
   The acceptance speech   52
   Television at the national conventions   52

7. Phase four: The campaign   54
   Campaign organization   54
   Campaign strategy   56
   Campaign tactics   59
     Raising money   59
     Spending money   61
     Allocating resources   62
     Making a new place for women   63
   Campaign finance   64
   Mass media in campaigning   69
     News media coverage   69
     Equal-time provisions   73
     Use of radio and TV by candidates   74

8. Phase five: The election   76
   The electoral college system   76
   Election day   81
   Reporting the results   82
   The final stages   84

Afterword   86

Appendix A: Provisions in the U.S. Constitution relating   88
   to the presidency
Appendix B: The presidential office   90
   • Qualifications for office • Term of office
   • Presidential oath of office
   • Salary • Duties and powers of the pres-
   ident • Succession to the presiden-
   cy • Vacancies in the vice-presidency
Appendix C: Presidential succession—are changes needed?   94
Appendix D: Constitutional amendments expanding   96
   the suffrage
Appendix E: Evolution of the presidential nomination   97
   process
Appendix F : 1980 electoral votes by state   99
Appendix G: Protection of candidates for the presidency   100
Appendix H: Significant presidential elections   100

Bibliography   102

1

On choosing the president

The president of the United States is probably the most important elected official in the world. The U.S. Constitution, political realities, and historical precedents combine to give the president a position in the American system of government unmatched by that of executives in other democratic countries. Indeed, even executives in nondemocratic countries may not be as strong. They must give considerable attention to the possibility of overthrow, while U.S. presidents rest secure in the knowledge that their power is based upon consent.

Over the years, the powers of the president as outlined in the Constitution have been fully utilized and even expanded by occupants of the office. The president has thus emerged as the chief political figure in the United States, despite the checks and balances implied by the separation of powers and the federal system. With a system of election that makes them the head of their political party and independent of the other branches of government, our presidents have usually won their battles with Congress, with the Supreme Court, and with the states.

Twentieth-century demands on government have further encouraged this trend. The president directly commands the large military forces of the nation and the major part of a vast civil bureaucracy. In addition, we expect the president to develop and push for legislation in areas of national concern, to serve as a symbol of the nation united, and even to establish and maintain trends in national morals and mores. Historically the key figure in

American foreign policy, the president, particularly over the past forty years, has had increasing influence in domestic policy as well. Whether negotiating a disarmament treaty, instituting wage controls, talking to astronauts on the moon, or commending an athlete, the president clearly affects the life of every person in America. The choosing of a president, then, is of great significance to every American, whether or not he or she participates in the process. (See Appendix A for constitutional provisions relating to the presidency.)

Television broadcasts of the national party conventions and candidate debates draw millions of people into the excitement of nominating and electing the president and vice-president. Some watch these proceedings only as spectators, as curious outsiders. Others feel the personal involvement that comes from understanding the entire process and/or having participated in it.

Only if one knows how political parties function and how they fit in the governmental structure can one understand fully how a presidential candidate becomes the party's official nominee. It helps, too, to know a few details about how the national conventions operate and how they are organized, how delegates are chosen, and how the convention actually nominates the candidates. The Federal Election Campaign Act (FECA) of 1971 as amended has made significant changes in the funding of federal elections. In this multimedia age it is also important to be aware of campaign techniques, strategies, and costs. Finally, the expansion of the franchise over the last decade suggests an even greater need to understand all phases of the election process, so that individuals can more clearly perceive how to be effective—how to have their voices heard in the choosing.

A president is elected only once every four years, but the *process* of election never really stops; it simply moves from one phase to another. Phase One, which could be called the preliminaries, extends roughly three years—from the presidential inauguration on January 20 to January 1 of the next presidential election year. This is the time for future presidential contenders to try to make a good record as officeholders, to become well known, to develop pockets of political strength, and to gain political commitments and endorsements. Phase Two begins with the election year and extends to the national conventions. Contenders now decide whether to become candidates and, if so, which primaries to enter. Delegates to the national conventions are selected during this period and candidates attempt to gain the support of as many as possible from every state. Phase Three covers the week or so that each national convention is in session. This can be a week of high drama as candidates for president and vice-president are finally nominated. Losing contenders at the convention may close ranks behind the winner, choose to sit out the election, or secede from their party and lead third-party movements of their own. Phase Four, the presidential campaign, extends from summer to early November. Phase Five encompasses the election itself, the formalization of the results, and the inauguration.

The presidential election does not take place in a vacuum but within the context of an existing political framework. In the United States that framework is provided by a system of institutionalized political parties and by a large and ever-changing electorate. Most presidential candidates are nominated by political parties, campaign as partisans, and are assisted to election by parties. At every stage in the election process the voters are called upon to make choices. They must assess the records of the various contenders, often express a preference in a precinct caucus or a primary, evaluate the convention choices, and vote on election day. Many citizens will also campaign on behalf of their choice in primary and election campaigns.

Choosing The President presents the political framework for presidential elections: first the political parties, then the voters; the five phases of the election process follow. The appendixes offer supplemental facts and figures.

2
The political framework: The parties

Though candidates have taken an increasingly nonpartisan pose over the years, all persons elected president since George Washington have run with the support of one of the two major parties of the period. In fact, the need to select an independent national executive was the chief impetus behind the rise of national parties. Once they were established, they continued to shape the process whereby presidents were chosen.

THE ROLE OF PARTIES[1]

Political parties perform a number of basic functions in a populous democratic country. Seen from the viewpoint of the voter, parties help clarify issues, relate candidates to these issues, and simplify the choices the citizen must make in elections. In addition, parties give some coherence to government and give the citizen a basis for judging the acts of that government. Without parties, citizens would have to find their way through a confusing maze of issues, candidates, and government actions. Seen from the viewpoint of political leaders, parties are the link between the three branches of the federal government and between local, state, and federal governments. They are also the means whereby party supporters are identified and mobilized behind candidates

---

[1]See V.O. Key, Jr., *Politics, Parties and Pressure Groups*, a standard work on American parties.

and programs. To use a familiar concept, parties are "brokers" that help to translate the wishes of people into government policy.

The American Constitution predates the rise of political parties; the document, therefore, makes no mention of them. Although now regulated by federal and state law, they have developed entirely as extraconstitutional bodies. As early as the 1790s, parties began to control the electoral college system and soon were exercising influence on all elections. Today, most federal and state office-holders, and many local ones as well, are chosen on a partisan basis. Despite this long history of party control of American politics, a popular belief in the desirability of being "nonpartisan" persists, based in part on an association (sometimes correct) of parties with "spoils" and corruption.

From the beginning, American politics has been dominated by two major parties. However, the constituencies of these parties have changed considerably over the years as some groups have defected from one party to another and new groups have had to be incorporated into the parties. The Democratic-Republicans of the Jefferson era were succeeded by the Democrats of Jackson's time, and that party continues today. The Federalists were followed by the Whigs, and the remnants of these groups, as well as new groups, were incorporated into the Republican party under Lincoln. For more than a hundred years, the Democratic and Republican parties have regularly contested national elections.

Traditionally in the United States, the two-party rather than a multiparty system has been considered the best way to choose a president: It simplifies the choice for voters. Recently, however, many political analysts have begun to question whether the two major political parties effectively address the needs and wants of voters and can appeal to virtually all segments of American society as they once did. Even before Vietnam, before Watergate, before recent economic recessions, increasing numbers of voters were identifying themselves as independents. And distrust and cynicism, which have increasingly come to characterize the attitudes of voters, have enlarged the numbers of political dropouts. These factors, most students of politics would sadly concede, are the setting for the 1980 elections.

There is considerable disagreement over what all this will mean for the American two-party system. Will the future bring a realignment[2] of constituents within the two major parties? Will it mean an entirely new party taking the place of the Democratic or Republican party? Or will it bring, more drastically, a breakdown into a multiparty system? Even those observers who think the two-party system will survive intact admit that the last decade has profoundly influenced how voters respond to the political system.

PARTY STRUCTURE

The structure of the official party organization has been likened to a layer cake—not a common layer cake, but an imposing wedding cake with at least four, sometimes five, distinct geographical tiers. The precincts are the bottom layer. At the top, instead of figures of the bride and groom, stands the figure of the chair of the national committee.

The titular heads of the parties are the president and the defeated nominee of the other party. But their positions are of varying importance in party organization. Some presidential candidates have had little influence during the four years following their defeat at the polls.[3]

As in a wedding cake, each tier of the party's organization is dependent on the layer below it. In addition, each tier, from precinct to national committee, has its special responsibility within its geographical area in the elections. A common cause, not a chain of command, elicits the necessary cooperation.

The following outline is a skeleton of the structure of the official organization of the two major political parties. The actual situation is far less tidy. Aside from the national committee, each party does not have a complete working organization at each level, except during election campaigns. In some precincts in some very large

---

[2]Realignment refers to lasting change in political behavior and party loyalties, generally in response to a stirring issue. Some political scientists believe there have been five major realignments in American political history. In 1800, the issue was the power of the national government; in 1828, Jacksonianism; in 1860, slavery; in 1896, monetary policy and capitalism; in 1932, the Depression. Michael Malbin, *National Journal*, May 31, 1975, p. 802.

[3]For an interesting description of post-1960 election events touching upon Nixon's claim to the titular leadership of the Republican party, see Paul T. David, "The Political Changes of 1960-61," *The Presidential Election and Transition 1960–61* (Washington, D.C.: Brookings Institution, 1961), pp. 327–28.

cities—even in some counties—no full organization exists for either major party.

Each of these political layers, including those not in the limelight during the nominating conventions, plays a vital role in choosing the nominees for, and in electing, the president and the vice-president.

The precinct, a neighborhood of hundreds of voters, is the basic unit in the political structure and the first theater of operation for party workers. The approximately 175,000 such units are headed by precinct captains or precinct leaders (other titles are also used). They may be chosen at caucuses, at direct primary elections, or in the general election; or they may be appointed by higher party officials. This precinct executive is the direct link between voters in the precinct and the professional political group. This is the party organization person who, through block workers and other aides, knows a great deal about the individual voters in the precinct and has substantial direct influence on them. Through this leader, the working members of the party at the precinct level, if they work hard in the party and are articulate at the right time and place, may make their voices heard in the selection of delegates.

The county committee, the party tier just above the precinct (in larger cities, just above the ward or district, which is composed of several precincts), is a unit of major significance in the party machinery. It consists of precinct executives or alternates chosen by them. The nation's 3,200-plus counties have greater reality as functioning political entities than do the congressional districts. Major decisions in the selection of congressional district delegates to the national conventions are often made at county level.[4] County committees are tied into the state organization through the county chairpersons, who direct precinct leaders in getting out the vote.

The state committee or state central committee forms the tier above the county committee. The state committeeman is an important party figure. The authority and composition of state committees are usually spelled out in state law. They range in size from a handful of people to hundreds of members. Methods of

---

[4]Paul T. David, Malcolm Moos, and Ralph M. Goldman, *Presidential Nominating Politics in 1952* (Baltimore: Johns Hopkins Press, 1954), p. 165.

selection differ widely from state to state. The chief function of state committees is to conduct campaigns through their officers and agents and to help in governing the party. They may also influence the choice of delegates to the national conventions, whatever the official selection process may be. In some cases the state committee still selects some delegates. Where states have conventions to select delegates, the state committee wields great influence. Even in states that select delegates via the primary method, control of the state committee may be extremely important.

The national committee is the top layer of party organization. This has representatives, at least one man and one woman, from each state and is of prime importance in the choosing of a president. Its chair is a top-ranking professional politician. Its powers and duties are dictated by the national convention.

"Kingpin of the national organization,"[5] the national committee chair is theoretically elected by the national committee but in practice is designated, immediately after the national convention, by the party's presidential candidate.

National committee members may be described as top politicians in their states. Although the national conventions must formally approve, they are in effect selected by the states, by a variety of methods. Two of the most common ways are election by the state convention and election by the state's delegates to the national convention. In a number of states, committee members are elected by the voters in the primary, and some state committees appoint the national members. They are usually wealthy, because membership on the national committee is costly in both time and money. Many combine experience in law, business, and politics.

The national committee members may be the unquestioned statewide party leaders, or their power may emanate from a densely populated area in the state. They may be close aides of the party leaders, or they may be getting their reward for generous contributions of money or for years of party service or distinction.

National committeewomen have usually been state or county vice-chairs of their parties. Until recently, they enjoyed little

---

[5]Key, *Politics, Parties and Pressure Groups*, p. 319.

power in their state parties, other than as reliable volunteers; and they had distinctly less status than their male counterparts on the national committees. This situation is beginning to change, though more in structure, so far, than in real power, as a result of efforts in both parties to increase women's participation.

Apart from its internal structure, each party also has a Senate Campaign Committee and a Congressional Campaign Committee, selected in each new Congress at conferences of party members. These committees raise funds and help in the campaigns of candidates for the Senate and the House of Representatives. Differences in the constituencies and in the election timetables frequently create enmity between these committees and the national committees.

OTHER POLITICAL GROUPS

In addition to the regular party organization in the United States, there are many auxiliary political groups, outside the formal party structure, which supplement the work of the regular party. There are those that appeal to special segments of the party membership—the National Federation of Republican Women and the Young Democrats, for example. Some groups are splinter groups or factions within the parties and may represent dissatisfaction with the regular leadership. The California Democratic Clubs, for instance, represented mostly former supporters of Adlai E. Stevenson opposed to the more traditional regular party leadership of Assembly Speaker Jesse Unruh.

The FECA requires that candidates for president who *either* receive more than $1,000 in contribution *or* spend more than $1,000 in a calendar year name a single organization as his or her campaign committee. The committee must keep track of all contributions to the candidate's campaign chest and all expenditures made in the candidate's name, and it must report these to the Federal Election Commission. These committees are not part of the regular party structure. They are personal committees with loyalties to one candidate only, not to the party to which the candidate belongs. Some knowledgeable observers point out that the FECA mandate to set up these independent committees outside the regular party apparatus is helping to increase the fragmentation of American political party organization.

A CLOSER LOOK AT THIRD PARTIES

Although American politics has been dominated by two major parties, "third" or minor parties have also played an important role in the party system.[6] They flourish whenever the electorate is deeply divided over issues, producing a vociferous minority. In the last decade, for example, conflicts over how to achieve integration have been catalysts for the reemergence of third parties, with candidates who pound away at issues, such as busing, on which the major parties take positions too "soft" to suit dissidents.

The Republican party was once a third party; the Populist party scarred the major parties in the 1890s; Theodore Roosevelt formed the "Bull Moose" party in the 1912 election; and in 1924 the Progressives, led by Robert M. La Follette, Sr., of Wisconsin, got 17 percent of the popular vote by addressing the issue of corporate domination.

In a few states there are third parties that are important at the state level but do not compete for national office; nonetheless, by forming coalitions they can wield considerable influence. In 1970 the Conservative party candidate, James L. Buckley, won the U.S. Senate race in New York.

In 1976 former Minnesota Senator Eugene J. McCarthy ran for president as an independent, but he lacked the funds, the national constituency, and the campaign organization to mount a strong candidacy.

Over the last forty years, only in 1968 has a third party made a significant impact in presidential electoral politics. In that year the American Independent Party, led by Governor George Wallace of Alabama, won 13.5 percent of the total popular vote. Wallace won more electoral votes than any third-party nominee in more than a century.

Following the assassination attempt in 1972 that put him in a wheelchair, Wallace was forced to alter his campaign tactics and techniques. As the 1976 presidential season rolled around, he also

---

[6]For a historical perspective on the growth of third parties, see Daniel A. Mazmanian, *Third Parties in Presidential Elections.*

changed his basic strategy. Seeking to legitimize his place in national politics and to avail himself of some of the opportunities offered by Democratic party reforms, he ran as a Democrat in the preliminaries.

3
The political framework: The voters

The efforts of the political parties and related political groups all point toward one objective—to bring to the polls on election day voters who will support their candidates. These voters, referred to as the electorate, form the second major part of the political framework for American presidential elections.

THE EXPANSION OF THE SUFFRAGE

The founding fathers did not have universal adult suffrage in mind as the power base of government, even though they were opposed to arbitrary rule and had faith in popular sovereignty. In fact, with few exceptions, the earliest years of our democracy gave the vote exclusively to white males who "had a stake in society" (owned property). By 1850, however, almost all the states had extended the right to vote—at least to all adult free males. Gradually, by constitutional amendment and by federal and state law, the base of democracy has widened and the country has moved steadily in the direction of universal adult suffrage.[1]

Since general voting qualifications were left to the states by the federal Constitution, constitutional amendments and federal statutes have often been employed to expand the electorate. States still set voting qualifications but they may not deny the franchise

---

[1]The close connection between democracy and voting is seen in the words *suffrage* and *franchise*. *Suffrage* comes from a Latin word meaning approval, while *franchise* is from an Old French word meaning freedom.

because of race (Fifteenth Amendment) or sex (Nineteenth Amendment). The most recently passed amendment, the Twenty-sixth, provides that anyone 18 years of age or over may not be denied the vote on the grounds of age. In addition, the Seventeenth Amendment allowed everyone to vote directly for United States senators for the first time, the Twenty-third allowed residents of the District of Columbia to vote for president, and the Twenty-fourth banned payment of a poll tax as a requirement for voting. Currently before the states is an amendment that would allow residents of the District of Columbia full voting representation in the Senate and House. These constitutional changes, together with early action by the states abolishing the initial property restrictions, have had the effect of extending the franchise to every segment of the population. (See Appendix D for text of amendments.)

VOTER TURNOUT AND PROCEDURAL PROBLEMS

Being *eligible* to vote, of course, is not the same as voting. Despite enfranchisement of people on a *group* basis, many *individuals* still do not vote. More people vote in presidential elections than in any other American election, yet even here the turnout rarely exceeds 65 percent of the voting-age population and is often lower. In 1972 about 12 million registered voters failed to vote; about 33 million eligible voters didn't even register. In 1976, only 54.4 percent of America's eligible voters turned out.

Since voting has never been compulsory in the United States, either in law or in fact, turnout depends on a wide range of motivating factors—one's sense of civic responsibility, one's estimate of how effective government is, even one's feelings of economic or physical safety. Still other factors keep people away from the polls—poor health, inadequate information about where and how to vote, and transportation problems, to name a few.

Apathy and dislike of politics in general or of the specific candidates play their part in these voting trends. Even traditionally active voters have begun to join the ranks of the younger, poorer, and less educated in turning away from the polls because they think their vote won't make much difference or because they don't care.

Motivation is put to the test in yet another important way: through procedural roadblocks on the way to the voting booth. American history has seen many examples of voting eligibility being given with one hand and taken away with the other by cumbersome voting procedures. Most states require registration in advance of voting, and the procedural problems at this stage have in the past been legion: prove residence in the state and precinct . . . prove you have paid poll taxes for several years . . . pass a long and complicated "literacy" test . . . convince the registrar of your good moral character. The hardy voter who cleared these hurdles could still find a long line at the polling place on election day and a long and confusing ballot in the voting booth.

Despite such barriers, persons with very high motivation still voted. Those who were somewhat less highly motivated or those for whom voting involved risks, however, often yielded to discouragement. Not surprisingly, voting turnout was lowest in the Deep South, where income levels were lowest, registration procedures most cumbersome, and racial discrimination most obvious.

Some of these obstacles to voting remain today, but there has been progress in eliminating them in recent years. After the Twenty-fourth Amendment in 1964 banned poll taxes in federal elections, the U.S. Supreme Court completed the task by declaring these taxes unconstitutional for state elections as well. Even more comprehensive are the Voting Rights Act of 1965 and its 1970 and 1975 amendments.

The 1965 Voting Rights Act

In counties that maintained a "test or device" as a prerequisite to registration or voting *and* had less than half their voting-age population registered or actually voting in the 1964 election, the act:

■ banned literacy tests (a provision aimed at some southern states that had used tests for purposes of racial discrimination);

■ required that federal examiners be sent out to protect voting rights; and

■ required federal approval of election law changes in areas covered by the act.

The 1970 Amendments:

- banned any test or device designed to examine the qualifications of a prospective voter in any election in the country;
- for presidential elections, limited states to 30-day residence rules and allowed residents who moved to use absentee ballots if they failed to meet the residency requirements of their new address; and
- reduced the voting age to 18 for all elections—national, state, and local. Later the Supreme Court upheld the lowering of the age for federal elections but narrowly overturned application of that provision to state and local elections. (Since that time the Twenty-sixth Amendment to the Federal Constitution has enfranchised 18-year-olds in all elections.)

The 1975 Amendments:

- extended the act for another seven years through mid-1982;
- made the ban on state literacy tests permanent; and
- mandated bilingual election materials and personal assistance as needed for voters whose primary language is not English. The foreign language aid is to be offered in designated counties and states where a significant voting-age population is found not to be proficient in the English language.

Earlier federal legislation had made absentee registration and voting easier for military and civilian government personnel outside the United States (1955) and then for all civilians overseas (1968, 1975, and 1978).

Despite the number of recently enacted reforms, a study by the Voter Education Project released in late 1975 concluded that millions of blacks in the South are still not registered to vote. Ten years after the Voting Rights Act, a broad gap between black and white voter registration remained in rural and urban counties, according to U.S. census data and official registration figures filed by Florida, Louisiana, North Carolina, and South Carolina. The Voter Education Project study maintains that government officials had been lax in encouraging blacks to vote and that inconvenient locations and hours continue to pose additional obstacles.

Though progress has been made, much remains to be done before the problem of registration procedures is solved. One proposal to encourage higher voter turnout in national elections by facilitating the registration process was a postcard registration plan. At least 18 states have established their own mail registration programs and can point to increased voter registration, but countrywide registration-by-mail does not seem to be just around the corner.

Another proposal, which would have effectively abolished registration requirements throughout the country, was introduced in Congress as part of a Carter-sponsored election reform package. Because of concern about possibilities of vote fraud, the bill never reached the House floor.

VOTER BEHAVIOR

Why people vote as they do has always been of interest to scholars, to candidates, and to political practitioners, such as the people who conduct polls or manage campaigns. Analysis of voting statistics and public opinion polls offers some tentative answers.

Party affiliation has long been regarded as the major factor determining votes in presidential elections, but there is recent evidence that party identification is declining. The belief that it is good to be an "independent voter" has been a popular one in the United States, even though independents dilute their voting effectiveness in many states because they have no voice in the process of nominating candidates. Being independent, rather than a party "captive," in an election would appear to be a reasonable way to preserve one's ability to vote on the basis of the candidate or the issue. The number of independents has risen dramatically in the last few years. While they were formerly thought to be the uneducated, many independents of the present period are new voters, young, and highly educated.[2]

The overwhelming majority of voters seldom think in terms of "liberal" and "conservative." They respond instead to particular

---

[2]A number of studies include research on this subject and reach similar conclusions. Among the best known are *The American Voter* by Angus Campbell et al. (see especially pages 143–45); Lester W. Milbrath's *Political Participation* (Chicago: Rand McNally and Co., 1965); and *The Voter Decides* by Angus Campbell, Gerald Gurin, and Warren Miller (Evanston: Peterson and Company, 1954). See also Robert D. Cantor, *Voting Behavior and Presidential Elections*.

issues. The personal qualities of candidates also influence voting behavior heavily, sometimes overriding the pull of party and issues. Dwight D. Eisenhower's presidential victories have been widely interpreted as an outstanding example. Long-term factors, such as ethnic background, occupation, and income, are always important, and religion has had a role in some American elections.

Although only 25 percent of the electorate identifies itself as Republican, Republican candidates have won four of the last seven presidential elections. Independents, who constitute about 37 percent of the electorate, have tended to support the Republican presidential candidates in recent elections. The remaining approximately 39 percent identifies itself as Democratic.[3] Lyndon B. Johnson managed to capture 56 percent of the independent vote, but Eisenhower and Richard M. Nixon got even higher percentages in their victories.

Ticket splitting is yet another factor that is having increasing impact. Voters may respond to state or local issues and candidates independently of presidential issues and candidates, or they may have strong emotional ties to one party at the local level but not at the national level. Nevertheless, despite the growing numbers of ticket splitters and independents, a voter's party identification is still believed to be a better determinant of how he or she will vote than any other factor. For example, blacks, who represent about 25 percent of the Democratic party's presidential electorate, tend to be the party's most loyal supporters and have on the whole backed Democratic candidates in the last four presidential elections.[4] Perhaps the most startling example of the ticket-splitting phenomenon in action occurred in 1972. For the first time in history, a president was elected with more than 60 percent of the popular vote without his party's gaining seats in the House and Senate or winning a majority in either congressional or gubernatorial elections.

A knowledge of voter behavior merely enables us to forecast political trends and group voting patterns broadly over a period of years. It does not allow us to foretell winners in every election or to predict the voting behavior of an individual.

---

[3]Based on the University of Michigan's Center for Political Studies party surveys.
[4]Ken Bode, "Black Democrats at the Tower of Babel," *New Republic.*

4
Phase one: The preliminaries

The three and a half years or so that elapse between actual presidential campaigns are not a respite from presidential politics but preliminaries to the main event. The political events that occur during this preliminary period will vary, depending upon whether the persons involved are members of the in-party (the party that controls the presidency) or the out-party, or parties.[1] However, all parties and all prospective candidates have to do three essential things in this period: establish a record that will make candidacy possible, develop a power base from which a candidacy can be launched, and devise a strategy to get the convention delegates necessary for nomination.

IN-PARTY PRELIMINARIES

The decisions of all prospective candidates in the in-party are heavily affected by the fact that a member of their party is in the White House. Historically, incumbent presidents have been hard to defeat in an election, and it was considered nearly impossible to wrest the nomination from them if they wanted it. However, it is generally conceded that Eugene McCarthy's strong showing in the 1968 New Hampshire Democratic primary greatly influenced

---

[1]The four books by Theodore H. White on the making of the president offer some of the best material available on the preliminary period.

Lyndon Johnson's decision not to seek his party's renomination. In 1976 former California Governor Ronald Reagan's challenge to President Gerald Ford's Republican candidacy also challenged historic precedent. Many observers thought that Ford's apparent vulnerability could be attributed to his being the first nonelected president in our history. Appointed to the vice-presidency before becoming president, he never had run for either office.

In the fall of 1979, supporters of Senator Edward Kennedy were urging him to consider challenging President Carter for the 1980 Democratic nomination. Were Carter to fail to be nominated, he would be the first sitting president seeking the nomination to be denied it since Chester A. Arthur was rejected by his party in 1884. Other incumbents to be so denied—all of them like Ford and Arthur had succeeded to the top slot from the vice-presidency— were John Tyler in 1844, Millard Fillmore in 1852, and Andrew Johnson in 1868.

Although a race between President Carter and Senator Kennedy may change the rules, it has been true in the past that whether a president seeks reelection or not, it is his presidential record that the in-party will carry into the next campaign. From a political standpoint a president must build a legislative, executive, and diplomatic record that will stand his party in good stead. Policy promises must be kept and political commitments fulfilled. Especially important to the in-party is the midterm election in which all House seats and a third of the Senate seats are filled. Historically, the in-party loses congressional seats in the midterm election. If losses are too heavy they will be interpreted as a repudiation of the president and his policies, so he has to work to minimize losses and maintain party morale. As the presidential election year approaches, he must pay even more attention to the likely political impact of his actions.

The presidency is the best power base from which to launch a candidacy. If the incumbent does not seek reelection, other candidates must use whatever sources of strength they have. In modern times, the vice-presidency seems to be a good spot for gaining a nomination, but not a particularly good one for winning an election. A vice-president has the advantage of executive experience and presidential support, but on the other hand he is stuck with the presidential record for better or worse. Since experience has shown that disunity is fatal, he must stand with the record and perhaps fall with it, as Vice-President Hubert Humphrey did in 1968. Governors, senators, and perhaps a former candidate may also come to the fore if a president steps down.

If a president decides to seek another term, his strategy during the preliminary period will be simple: maintain party harmony and make sure he controls enough party machinery to ensure that the convention will be a mere formality, renominating him by acclamation and stoutly defending his policies. In the past, the decision of whether to dump an incumbent vice-president came at a later stage. Nelson A. Rockefeller's vow early in the 1976 race not to run with Ford may set a new pattern in motion.

If a president steps down, other contenders will have many decisions to make: when to announce their candidacy, how heavily to lean on the president in winning delegates, how to use presidential primaries, etc. In 1968 Sen. Robert F. Kennedy tried to win nomination through the primary route; Senator McCarthy mounted an extensive grassroots campaign effort; Vice-President Humphrey worked behind the scenes with presidential support. By and large, in-party strategies are determined by circumstances, the most important of which is the position taken by the incumbent president.

OUT-PARTY PRELIMINARIES

Presidential contenders in the out-party (or parties) are in a position quite different from that of their in-party counterparts and may even have an advantage if the president does not seek reelection. Since they have not been responsible for broad legislative programs, executive actions, or diplomatic initiatives, they can criticize presidential efforts in all areas. Even if the out-party controls the Congress, an individual aspirant cannot be held to account because the out-party does not develop a broad legislative program of its own, responding instead to presidential actions.

To be sure, a presidential hopeful must build a creditable *individual* record. A governor or mayor who is a contender will, of course, have one. But the record can be, and often is, more in the nature of promises than accomplishments.

To build a record at all, an out-party aspirant needs a power base.

Although candidacies are sometimes launched from appointive positions (Eisenhower in 1952) or private law practices (Nixon in 1968), an elective office is considered best. A party's "titular leader" (most recent losing presidential candidate) will probably try to gain such a position as soon as possible. After 1968, Humphrey sought and obtained his old Senate seat from Minnesota at the first opportunity; after 1972, George McGovern concentrated on retaining his Senate seat from South Dakota.

Because of the power and prestige of the position and the modern importance of international affairs, the Senate, rather than state or local government, in recent years has been a good spot for individuals with presidential ambitions. In 1976, however, candidates from many different arenas emerged. Of the 11 announced Democratic presidential contenders at the start of the campaign season, only four were senators: Henry M. Jackson (WA), Birch Bayh (IN), Lloyd M. Bentsen (TX), and Robert C. Byrd (WV). A fifth, Fred R. Harris (OK), was a former senator. Of the six other candidates, two were former governors, Jimmy Carter (GA) and Terry Sanford (NC); two were sitting governors, Milton J. Shapp (PA) and George C. Wallace (AL); one was a representative, Morris K. Udall (AZ); and one, R. Sargent Shriver, had been the Democrats' vice-presidential nominee in 1972.

In the earliest stages of the "prelims," contenders try to build a favorable image in the party and in the country by making frequent public speeches and appearances at party functions. If prospects seem bright and financial backing emerges, this period of active "noncandidacy" will be followed by a formal announcement. The FECA discourages the formerly common practice of front-runners waiting until the last minute to announce their entry into the race. Limits on the size of campaign contributions mean that those who start raising money early have an advantage.

In the past, some contenders did not engage in preliminary campaigning at all but waited to be "drafted." These drafts were rarely genuine; rather, they were matters of strategy.[2] (The proliferation of primary elections—at least 35 in 1980—may make the possibility of draft candidacies unlikely.) Sometimes contenders—usually front-runners—use a middle-of-the-road appeal

---

[2]See Walter Johnson, *How We Drafted Adlai Stevenson.*

to broaden their base of support, while still others look to particular groups for support.

Whether to make a vigorous attack on the presidential record is always an important question, the choice usually being dictated by the contender's past record in this regard and by the current popularity of the incumbent. When a president's popularity ebbs, contenders are more inclined to play on antigovernment themes, as was the case in the 1976 contest.

The final strategy decision centers on how to handle the building of delegate strength for the nominating convention. At this point, some of the earlier hopefuls will withdraw because they have failed to get enough money or other support, and the field will be left to those with the most serious chances of success.

THE MEDIA IN THE PRELIMINARIES

The mass media, particularly television and the national newspapers and magazines, play an important role in the preliminary stage of presidential elections.[3] They can create a front-runner by giving him exposure or by declaring that he is the front-runner. If they do not take a candidacy seriously, it will be much harder for the contender to raise money and capture early delegate commitments. A president who is a candidate has great advantages in media access. The president is news and gets coverage accordingly, and it seems impossible to nullify this built-in advantage. In recent years the out-party has tried, with only limited success, to get free television time to answer telecast presidential statements of a partisan flavor. In both 1972 and 1976, however, the networks did provide the Democratic party with prime time to respond to the incumbent president's State of the Union address.

Charges of bias in the media are common and come from all sides. One of Vice President Spiro T. Agnew's first "official" acts was to denounce the media for their handling of President Nixon's program. Governor Wallace regularly complained that the media distorted his views.

During the 1972 campaign, Senator Edmund S. Muskie (D-ME) bitterly protested the way the press treated him; after his famous

---

[3]For one study, see Edward W. Chester, *Radio, Television and American Politics.*

"emotional" scene outside the *Manchester Union Leader* offices, some political commentators who covered the campaign say Muskie never regained his stature as a credible candidate. On the other hand, a member of the 1976 Carter staff argued that Carter's *unfavorable* press coverage meant that he was finally being taken seriously.

Rep. Shirley A. Chisholm (D,L-NY), the first black woman to seek the presidential nomination, was never really taken seriously by the press. The political clout she developed during the 1972 campaign was a shocker to all concerned; yet most members of the press corps made no mention that she might pose a threat to other better-known liberal candidates.

Even incumbents are sensitive to the make-or-break powers of the media in the early stages of campaigning, when most of the jockeying for early support goes on. In early 1976, President Ford seemed to feel he was "under the gun" from the press. According to president-watcher David Broder of the *Washington Post*, Ford responded by striking a "defiant" pose and staunchly defending some of his more controversial policies.

5

Phase two: Delegate selection – the convention game begins

It's a lot more exciting to watch candidates on the campaign trail than it is to read the fine print that governs who gets to go to the conventions where nominees are chosen. But this has always been important, and perhaps even more so in 1980, because campaign laws and new party rules are overturning old alliances and accustomed dominations. There are new referees whose real power is being tested—as is the case with the Democrats' Compliance Review Commission. Even the pros can't follow the game without a scorecard.

The process was never simple, partly because the methods used to choose delegates vary from state to state and between the two major parties. What follows is an outline of the two basic systems, the convention or caucus and the primary, plus a chart of state-by-state information.

METHODS OF CHOOSING DELEGATES

All systems are based on two general methods: (1) the convention or caucus and (2) the primary. Many states use a combination of conventions and primaries—selecting some delegates one way and some another. In most systems, people who want to be delegates may commit themselves to a specific presidential candidate or they may run uncommitted.

The convention/caucus

Under this method of selection, delegates are chosen by party conventions. The process begins when party members meet in grassroots local caucuses (usually at precinct level) to select delegates to the next level (usually the county). The county conventions then choose delegates to go to the congressional district and state conventions. In most cases, these state delegates may meet in their own congressional districts to select some of the national delegates before going on to meet with the whole state convention to select the rest. Under the rules of the Democratic party, at each point in the process the presidential preferences of the delegates chosen to go to the next level should fairly reflect the proportion of people attending the caucus or convention who are committed to each presidential candidate or who are uncommitted. There is one limit on this right: Each state sets a minimum percentage of the vote, below which the right to representation is lost. For some states it is 15 percent, for others as low as 10 or 5 percent. The exact sequence of meetings, the dates, and the format used vary from state to state.

The primary

In a primary, party members express their preferences through an election, rather than by attending a meeting or caucus. In the civics textbooks, primaries appear to be an ideal expression of democracy in action, an opportunity for voters to show their support for major party contenders. In real life, however, primaries haven't worked quite that way. Most candidates discover that the primary route to the presidency is a grueling marathon for an elusive prize.[1]

Primaries were devised in the early twentieth century during the reformist Progressive era as a way to take power away from party bosses and make politics more democratic and closer to the people. By 1916, 26 states had primary laws on the books, though only some of them applied to the presidential nomination. By 1935 eight states had repealed their primary laws, but after World War II interest in primaries revived. In 1976 the number of primaries was 31. In 1980 there will be 36. Few states, however, use the primary by itself.

Ironically, in 1976 those candidates with the skimpiest budgets chose to push themselves in the earliest primary, that in New Hampshire. As David Broder explained it, "The real prize for

[1]Elizabeth Drew, "Running," *New Yorker*.

Types of Primaries

Although primaries vary greatly, there are only three basic types that affect delegate selection: the winner-take-all, the proportional, and the direct delegate selection primary.* The major distinction between primary systems is whether delegates are allocated on the basis of votes cast for presidential candidates or on the basis of votes cast for the delegates themselves. In both the winner-take-all and the proportional primaries, the outcome is decided by how many votes the *presidential candidates* themselves receive.

Winner-take-all primaries: The presidential candidate receiving the most votes gets *all* of the delegates to be allocated through the primary. The names of the delegates might appear in slates on the ballot along with the candidate, or they might actually be chosen by another method (such as convention) and be bound to vote for whichever candidate wins. The Democrats have outlawed the winner-take-all primary, but the Republicans will have nine.

Proportional primary: Works much the same way as "winner-take-all," with votes for presidential candidates themselves determining the outcome. However, instead of one presidential candidate getting them all, delegates are divided among candidates in proportion to the percentage of votes that each candidate receives. A candidate who gets 60 percent of the primary vote gets 60 percent of the delegates. One who gets 20 percent of the vote gets 20 percent of the delegates, etc. The specific delegates assigned to each candidate on the basis of the primary are usually chosen by one of the other nonprimary methods of delegate selection and pledged to that candidate. Twenty-nine Democratic and 15 Republican proportional primaries are scheduled.

Direct delegate selection primary: Votes for the delegates themselves, rather than for presidential candidates, determine the outcome. The delegates who get the most votes win and are sent to the national convention. However, in nearly all states the presidential preference of the delegates is indicated on the ballot, so it is easy for voters to express their presidential preferences by voting only for delegates pledged to that candidate. If all delegates who win are committed to the same candidate, the effect is the same as in the winner-take-all.

Although the Democrats have outlawed the winner-take-all primary, they do allow direct delegate selection primaries if the primary is conducted at the smaller congressional district level rather than statewide. So even if all the delegates for a particular candidate win in one congressional district, another candidate might still pick up delegates in a different part of the state. Nevertheless, this kind of primary in the Democratic party has been nicknamed the "loophole primary" by those who feel it undercuts the party's intent to eliminate the winner-take-all situation. In 1980, direct delegate selection will be used only in conjunction with the advisory primaries.

---

*Several states will have advisory primaries that are totally unrelated to delegate selection. These "beauty contests" merely let voters express their presidential preferences so delegates chosen some other way will know how the public feels.

those hungry Democrats is not the 17 votes—barely 1 percent of the 1,505 votes needed for nomination—but a chance for an inexpensive early victory that could draw new money into their dollar-starved campaigns."

Generally, early primaries are important in narrowing the field of candidates, while midseason and late primaries finally resolve the intraparty contests.

Some primaries involve semicandidates known as favorite sons—often state governors or acknowledged state party leaders who may not even have an organized campaign staff but want to control their delegations and keep them unpledged. In most cases, they don't consider themselves real contenders. A variant on this technique is called the stalking horse. Here a political candidate appears to campaign on his or her own behalf but in fact seeks to divide the opposition or to conceal the identity of another contender.[2]

CRITIQUES OF THE PRIMARY SYSTEM

Do primaries actually give "power to the people," as their initiators expected? In 1976 only about 25 percent of the voting age population voted in primaries. Of these about two-thirds voted Democratic. This means that Carter won the Democratic nomination with the support of roughly 7 percent of the voting age population in primary states—or about 5 percent of the entire voting age population. Of the voters who turn out for primaries, most are better educated, more affluent, and older than those who vote in general elections.[3] They are also more likely to be interested in a particular candidate or to have strong party ties.

Primaries offer relatively unknown candidates a chance to build their credibility and to assess their general popularity and intraparty strength, but they can end unhappily for candidates who flunk this first exam. Party loyalists quail at the damage done to party cohesiveness by the in-fighting a primary contest always sets off and believe, moreover, that only "big name" candidates have a chance to score, although the successful candidacy of "unknown" Jimmy Carter seems to have softened some of this criticism.

[2]Leon W. Blevens, *The Young Voters Manual.*
[3]Richard M. Scammon, *America Votes*, vol. 10.

Delegate selection by state

Key

Types of Delegate Selection Processes

Primary P: Proportional; WTA: Winner-take-all; DD: Direct delegate selection; A: Advisory. (Approximately 75 percent of delegates in both parties are selected from states with primaries.)
Convention/Caucus (C/C): Congressional district convention, state convention, state committee, delegate caucus, or other variation.

State	Number of Delegate Votes*	Prevailing Type of Selection Process	Date of Primary, if Applicable	State	Number of Delegate Votes*	Prevailing Type of Selection Process	Date of Primary, if Applicable
ALABAMA				**INDIANA**			
D	45	P	March 1	D	80	P	May 6
R	27	P	March 1	R	54	WTA	May 6
ALASKA				**IOWA**			
D	11	C/C	—	D	50	C/C	—
R	19	C/C	—	R	37	C/C	—
ARIZONA				**KANSAS**			
D	29	C/C	—	D	37	P	April 1
R	28	C/C	—	R	32	P	April 1
ARKANSAS				**KENTUCKY**			
D	33	P	May 27	D	50	P	May 27
R	19	C/C	—	R	27	P	May 27
CALIFORNIA				**LOUISIANA**			
D	306	P	June 3	D	51	P	April 5
R	168	WTA	June 3	R	31	P	April 5
COLORADO				**MAINE**			
D	40	C/C	—	D	22	C/C	—
R	31	C/C	—	R	21	C/C	—
CONNECTICUT				**MARYLAND**			
D	54	P	March 25	D	59	P	May 13
R	35	P	March 25	R	30	WTA	May 13
DELAWARE				**MASSACHU-**			
D	14	C/C	—	**SETTS**			
R	12	C/C	—	D	111	P	March 4
DISTRICT OF				R	42	P	March 4
COLUMBIA				**MICHIGAN**			
D	19	P	May 6	D	141	A	May 20
R	14	WTA	May 6	R	82	P	May 20
FLORIDA				**MINNESOTA**			
D	100	P	March 11	D	75	C/C	—
R	51	WTA	March 11	R	34	C/C	—
GEORGIA				**MISSISSIPPI**			
D	63	P	March 11	D	32	C/C	—
R	36	WTA	March 11	R	22	C/C	—
HAWAII				**MISSOURI**			
D	19	C/C	—	D	77	C/C	—
R	14	C/C	—	R	37	C/C	—
IDAHO				**MONTANA**			
D	17	A	May 27	D	19	P	June 3
R	21	P	May 27	R	20	A	June 3
ILLINOIS				**NEBRASKA**			
D	179	A,DD	March 18	D	24	P	May 13
R	102	A,DD	March 18	R	25	A,DD	May 13

State	Number of Delegate Votes*	Prevailing Type of Selection Process	Date of Primary, if Applicable	State	Number of Delegate Votes*	Prevailing Type of Selection Process	Date of Primary, if Applicable
NEVADA				**TENNESSEE**			
D	12	P	May 27	D	55	P	May 6
R	17	P	May 27	R	32	P	May 6
NEW HAMPSHIRE				**TEXAS**			
				D	152	C/C	—
D	19	P	Feb. 26	R	80	WTA	May 3
R	22	P	Feb. 26	**UTAH**			
NEW JERSEY				D	20	C/C	—
D	113	P	June 3	R	21	C/C	—
R	66	A,DD	June 3	**VERMONT**			
NEW MEXICO				D	12	A	March 4
D	20	P	June 3	R	19	A***	March 4
R	22	P	June 3	**VIRGINIA**			
NEW YORK				D	64	C/C	—
D	282	P	March 25	R	51	C/C	—
R	123	**	March 25	**WASHINGTON**			
NORTH CAROLINA				D	58	C/C	—
				R	37	C/C	—
D	69	P	May 6	**WEST VIRGINIA**			
R	40	P	May 6	D	35	A,DD	June 3
NORTH DAKOTA				R	18	A,DD	June 3
D	14	C/C	—	**WISCONSIN**			
R	17	C/C	—	D	75	P	April 1
OHIO				R	34	WTA	April 1
D	161	P	June 3	**WYOMING**			
R	77	WTA	June 3	D	11	C/C	—
OKLAHOMA				R	19	C/C	—
D	42	C/C	—	**PUERTO RICO**			
R	34	C/C	—	D	41	P	March 16
OREGON				R	14	WTA	February 17
D	39	P	May 20	**VIRGIN ISLANDS**			
R	29	P	May 20	D	4	C/C	—
PENNSYL-VANIA				R	4	C/C	—
D	185	P	April 22	**GUAM**			
R	83	A,DD	April 22	D	4	C/C	—
RHODE ISLAND				R	4	C/C	—
D	23	P	June 3	**LATIN AMERICAN REGIONAL DEMOCRATS**			
R	13	P	June 3		4	C/C	—
SOUTH CAROLINA							
D	37	C/C	—	**DEMOCRATS ABROAD**	4	—	—
R	25	WTA	March 1				
SOUTH DAKOTA							
D	19	P	June 3				
R	22	A	June 3				

TOTALS: Democrats: 3,331 votes; Republicans: 1,994 delegates and votes.

*   In the Republican party, this column represents the total number of delegates from that state, as each delegate has one vote. In the Democratic party, the number of delegate votes may be less than the number of delegates, because states entitled to fewer than 16 allocated delegates may elect 16 delegates to share those votes. The Latin American Regional Democrats, Guam, the Virgin Islands, and Democrats Abroad may elect 8 delegates each to cast the votes to which they are entitled.

**   In the New York state Republican primary, delegates are elected with no indication of presidential preference and are not bound to a particular candidate.

*** In Vermont, 10 of the state's 19 delegates are awarded to the top vote-getter in the primary—if that candidate receives at least 40 percent of the vote.

Critics of the primary system observe that the process rewards the most effective campaigner—who may not be the most effective president. These observers also point out that the primary system makes unreasonable and burdensome demands on candidates, that candidates who are most successful are in danger of ruining their health, and that the elected officials among them, in particular, are prone to neglect their obligations. Still other critics say that with so many primaries, candidates are spread too thin. They have too little time to address the issues, and voters have too little chance to assess the candidates' relative merits and deficiencies. The litany goes on: too much is made of winning big, or at least making a respectable showing, and it all adds up to too much money, too much time spent away from pressing matters, and inefficient use of resources.

Proposals for reform of this stage of the nomination process include revitalizing the role of party professionals in selecting nominees and constitutional amendments establishing a national primary or bringing about more uniformity among the state primaries (e.g., by standardizing the timetable and thereby shortening the time span). Both proposals have shortcomings. No one seriously wants to go back to "smoke-filled rooms." A shortened primary period might mean that candidates would have even less time than they now do to speak out on issues and to make themselves known to the voters. Opponents of the national primary fear that it would be virtually impossible for candidates to campaign in every state. Regional primaries are still another proposed reform. But the argument against this approach is that it would distort the public's view of both issues and candidates.

All these options have been thrashed about for some time. It remains to be seen whether a consensus for major change will develop.

DEMOCRATIC PARTY REFORM

The Democratic party has spent a good deal of time in the interval since the 1968 convention in reforming its rules. So drastic were the changes in the makeup of delegate bodies selected under the rules developed by the McGovern-Fraser Commission for the 1972 convention that 31 states had their delegations challenged. That commission had been appointed to find ways to democratize the process of delegate selection after the cataclysmic events of the 1968 Democratic convention. Its two most controversial rules (1) encouraged more participation by and representation of young people, women, and racial minorities by imposing *quotas* and (2) limited the number of delegates selected by state party committees to 10 percent of the total delegation. For the 1976 convention the Mikulski Commission wrote a new set of rules governing selection of delegates, modifying many of the 1972 reforms. Quotas were replaced by affirmative action programs, and the portion of delegates that state party committees may select has been upped from 10 to 25 percent.

The Compliance Review Commission (CRC), first used in 1976, prescreens challenges or penalizes state delegations that fail to comply with the rules governing participation of women, the young, the elderly, or minority groups.

The Democrats have continued to make significant changes in their rules for the 1980 convention:

- State delegations must be equally divided between men and women.
- The time period when delegates may be chosen has been shortened to three months—from the second Tuesday in March to the second Tuesday in June.
- Only registered Democrats may vote in Democratic primaries.
- State delegations must reflect the proportion of the vote each candidate receives in the primary election or state caucuses.
- The number of delegates is increased by 10 percent to allow elected party and state officials to be included.

The Democrats' new rules make it harder than in the past for a candidate to capture a first-ballot nomination victory, because abolition of winner-take-all primaries means that a larger number of presidential candidates will go to the national convention with some delegates pledged to their candidacies for at least one ballot; obversely, it will be almost impossible for any candidate to go to the convention with a whole state delegation pledged. The reforms will also change the format of the convention, alter the composition of the delegate bodies, affect campaign strategy, and encourage the proliferation of favorite son candidates who might be able to exert influence on the selection of the party's nominee.

REPUBLICAN PARTY REFORM

Republican reforms have been more cautious than those of the Democrats. They speak, for example, of "positive action" rather than of the Democrats' "affirmative action," (itself a retreat from "quotas"), and they provide no enforcement mechanism.

Like the Democrats, the GOP created a panel after the 1972 convention to make recommendations for reform in the party's rules. The "Rule 29 Committee" produced few proposals for substantive changes, and even fewer were accepted by the national party leadership. Minor reforms included a ban on proxy voting and on ex-officio or automatic "senior party official" delegates. The fate of efforts to do away with the "bonus vote" provision is discussed in Chapter VI.

Going into the 1980 convention, Republicans have no equivalent to the CRC. Reliance is entirely on voluntary compliance, a posture signaled by the use of "should" rather than "shall" in all reform rules. The small semantic difference could have a large influence on the state parties' response to the new national party rules.

6
Phase three: The national nominating conventions

"Several thousand people, most of them parochial in outlook and strangers to one another . . . thrown together for a few days to make a set of major decisions, under conditions of great strain and maximum publicity."[1] That's how one of the best writers on the subject describes the quadrennial rite of the national party conventions. Months of state convention and primary work and months or even years of candidate activity have gone before.

Well in advance of the meeting date, the national committees select an American city for the convention site. Local pride and the prospect of increased business induce many cities to lobby for the honor, and the national committees make their selections on the basis of convenience, available accommodations, and sometimes political considerations. In 1980 the Republican convention will convene on July 14 in Detroit, the Democratic convention on August 11 in New York City. The thousands of delegates, political leaders, newsmen, and tourists at work and play make convention weeks American festivals, but they are festivals with a serious purpose.

The functions of national conventions

National conventions have no legal standing. They represent only the particular sentiments of the party holding the convention. But make no mistake: They are exercises in power, though not

---

[1] Judith N. Parris, *The Convention Problem*, p. 4.

always on the floor of the convention hall. State laws and party rules regulate the process of delegate selection, but the conventions themselves are largely unregulated by state and federal law. They make their own rules and are the supreme authority over other parts of the national parties, including the national committees. They have few ways to enforce their mandates, however, short of denying admittance to a violator at a future convention, and must depend largely on voluntary compliance. Compliance is usually forthcoming, at least to a large degree, because without the work done by the national conventions, there could be no true national parties.

The convention performs four major functions for the party:

1. It nominates candidates for president and vice-president. The nominees can usually depend on having their names and/or a slate of electors pledged to them on the November election ballot in all the states, a luxury not easy for a minor party to come by. Though formal nomination is not a *legal* requirement, it is a practical necessity brought on by the development of a mass electorate. Although candidates could be nominated in a national primary, there are those who believe that this method of nomination would rob the conventions of their most important function and weaken the national parties by weakening their chief binding force.

2. It adopts a national party platform. Although the platform is certainly not binding on all members of the party, it does establish a certain tone and direction behind which most party members may rally, at least during the election, and serves a number of other purposes (see the section later in this chapter on committee work). After the election, presidents, representatives, and senators interpret the platform to suit their own needs and philosophies.

3. It governs the party. Policies and procedures for the next convention are determined and study groups, such as the commissions discussed earlier, may be appointed. Each state's nomination for national committeeman and committeewoman must be approved by the national convention. The party is thus provided with a new national committee to tend to party affairs for the next four years.

4. It serves as a campaign rally. The outbursts against the opposition serve as the first shots of the election campaign and help to build morale among the rank and file. The hoopla surrounding the conventions helps to heal wounds that may have been opened in the factional struggle over the nomination. The national conventions have never been mere business meetings at which candidates were nominated but national party "happenings" with a variety of functions.

THE GATHERING OF THE DELEGATES

A convention city on the eve of a convention is a hubbub of activity and expectancy. The delegates have been selected and are on their way, large delegations from distant states often traveling together. They may have held a meeting before leaving and have chosen a delegation chair, vice-chair, and secretary, or they may wait until they reach the convention city to organize and elect their leadership. Delegates in the past have usually been upper-middle-class, college-educated, professional or managerial, to some degree professional politicians—and mostly male. But as a result of party reforms, the mix has changed. Frequently, the delegates are politicians on the local or state level only and are not well known elsewhere. They may even have had only a limited previous connection with members of their own delegation.

Within minutes after delegates have checked in at hotels, the preliminary conferences and caucuses start. Each state has its own headquarters and calls its delegation together. Some are closed caucuses, while others are open to the presidential contenders and their representatives. Meeting at the same time are representatives of the major pressure groups—labor, business, agriculture, professional groups, religious groups, citizen groups—who hope to influence delegates in the choice of candidates and in the content of the party platform. Most of these groups will already have testified at earlier hearings of the platform committees. Television cameras, microphones, and amplifiers are everywhere in evidence in the convention hall as the party's national chair steps to the podium to open the proceedings. The hall and its galleries are filled as delegates, alternates, and visitors take their seats in the places assigned by the national committee. With a burst of drama—banners, emblems, music, and party fervor—the gavel goes down and the convention begins.

CONVENTION MAKEUP

Long before convention time each party will have decided two basic questions about the convention's size: how many people, voting delegates or otherwise, will be admitted to the convention in an official capacity and how the total number will be apportioned among the states. The allocation is determined by each party's national committee under authority granted at the last convention and is announced before the presidential election year.

Critics have often complained that the thousands of people in attendance at conventions make meaningful deliberation impossible. They have recommended smaller conventions with fewer delegate votes and fewer alternates (i.e., substitute delegates who step in if official delegates cannot fulfill their function for any reason). Most party leaders have argued, however, that there must be enough delegate votes to be representative of the nation as a whole. In addition, if the number of persons attending conventions were drastically reduced, it would reduce the number of faithful party workers who could be rewarded with a trip to the national convention.[2] These considerations have kept the national conventions large.

In 1980 over 5,400 persons will attend the Democratic party convention—3,331 delegates, 2,045 alternates, and others. The Republican convention will be smaller than the Democrats' and smaller than it was in 1976, with fewer than 2,000 voting delegates and a like number of alternates.

In apportioning delegate votes to the states, the national parties have been generally guided by two considerations: the population of the state and the voting strength of the party in the state. Population has been loosely recognized by basing much of a state's delegate allocation on its number of electoral votes (senators plus representatives); voting strength has been recognized by giving "bonus" delegates to the states where the party has recently done well.

The bonus system works like a mirror for both parties. Carter's

---

[2]Rewarded only in the sense of being designated as delegates, since in most states delegates must pay for their own transportation to and from the conventions as well as for their expenses while in attendance.

strength in the South means that states in that region will gain more delegates to the Democratic convention than any other region. The opposite is true for the Republican convention: Southern states will lose the largest number of delegates. Other states will lose substantial numbers of delegate votes in the Republican convention as a result of their ending up in the Democratic column in 1976. New York has 31 fewer delegates in 1980 than in 1976; Ohio, Pennsylvania, and Texas will lose 20; Florida will lose 15.

The national GOP's bonus vote system recently survived a strong challenge. The Ripon Society, an organization of young Republican liberals, argued that this system discriminates unfairly against larger states by reducing their influence. Specifically, California, with nearly 10 percent of the nation's population, got only 7.5 percent of the 1976 national convention delegates; New York, with 9 percent of the population, got only 6.8 percent of the delegate vote. After a series of truncated court battles, the U.S. Court of Appeals for the District of Columbia in effect upheld the old formula by saying that under the First Amendment political parties can manage their own affairs without interference from the courts. The ruling means that delegates need not be apportioned among states on a one-person-one-vote basis. An appeal to the Supreme Court was unsuccessful.

A frequently expressed criticism of the makeup of the 1976 Democratic convention was that too few experienced party officials and elected state officials were delegates. Therefore, in 1978 the Winograd Commission recommended a 10 percent expansion of each delegation to accommodate these officials. These "automatic" delegates, to be elected either by a state convention or by the remainder of the national convention delegation, are to be selected from the Democratic governor (if there is one), the state party chair and vice-chair, other members of the Democratic National Committee, and U.S. senators and representatives. For the first convention presidential candidate ballot, the "automatic" delegates vote for the choice of the state's primary or convention.

During the convention, the importance of the delegates varies, depending on the strength of the various presidential contenders and the unity within the party. If one contender is out front with a large number of assured delegate votes, as is usually the case when an incumbent president seeks renomination, the delegates play a passive role of consent during the convention. If it is a tight race, the delegates play the decisive role. If in addition to having a front-running candidate the convention produces little disagreement over platform matters, it is likely to be a quiet one.

Whenever the first few ballots fail to produce a winning nominee, a deadlocked or "brokered" convention develops. Brokered conventions are those in which party leaders and presidential candidates fight, negotiate, and compromise before they agree on a nominee. Not since 1952 has either party required more than one ballot to choose a presidential nominee. But many political observers are convinced that this time around it could take either party as many as two dozen ballots, or even 103 (as was the case with the Democrats in 1924), to get one candidate over the top. The federal matching funds, which are provided to candidates for president under public financing provisions of the FECA and are likely to encourage candidates to stay in the race until the bitter end, have been cited as an additional reason to expect a brokered convention.

COMMITTEE WORK

Much of the preliminary work of the conventions is done by committees. There are four in the Republican party: *Credentials, Resolutions (Platform), Rules and Order of Business,* and *Permanent Organization.* The Democrats have only three standing committees: *Platform, Rules,* and *Credentials:* a fourth, *Arrangements,* administers the operations end of the convention.

Republican party

The Republicans will retain their practice of having one man and one woman serve on each committee and will also allow each state, the District of Columbia, Puerto Rico, the Virgin Islands, and Guam one delegate representative. If a delegation is too small for a man and a woman to serve on all convention committees, then the delegation may allocate their appointments in any way they wish.

The *Credentials Committee* receives and monitors credentials of all delegates and alternates and determines the permanent roll of the convention. If there is to be a contest, it is resolved by the Republican National Committee up to one week prior to the convention.

The *Resolutions (Platform) Committee* drafts the party platform for the following four years. Months before the convention begins, research is begun and preliminary work gets under way with subcommittees on various issues established.

The *Committee on Rules and Order of Business* drafts the rules to be adopted by the convention, those pertaining to proceedings, organization of the national committee, and membership in the next convention.

The *Permanent Organization Committee* recommends a set of ongoing officers for the convention, the most important of whom is the permanent chair.

Democratic party

The party's standing committees have 158 members with 154 votes. The votes are allocated among states and territories by the same formula used to determine the size of national convention delegations; membership from each state or territory must be equally divided between men and women. Committee members are chosen by delegations to represent their presidential preferences proportionally. This procedure results in fractional voting. Members of the standing committees need not be delegates or alternates to the national convention. Meetings are open to the public.

Each standing committee may by majority vote determine additional rules of procedure required to do its work, if these rules don't clash with general convention rules.

The *Platform Committee* prepares the party platform with the input of *all* presidential candidates invited. A minority report can reach the floor, but only if 25 percent of the committee agrees.

The *Rules Committee* recommends the permanent rules of the convention, the agenda, the permanent officers of the convention, and amendments to the charter of the party and offers resolutions germane to anything not considered by the other convention committees.

The *Credentials Committee* determines and resolves questions involving delegates chosen for the convention, but the convention itself has ultimate authority over resolution of all credentials challenges, particularly those relating to challenges over failure to implement affirmative action plans. For all practical purposes, then, a delegation could be challenged at the convention itself.

The Democrats' guidelines on convention procedures retain 1972 reforms with minor modifications. Key features:

■ The grounds for credentials challenges have been narrowed and the power of the Credentials Committee chair broadened.

■ To bring a minority position to the floor for debate, 25 percent (vs. 10 percent in 1972) of the Credentials, Platform, or Rules Committee, whichever is involved, must approve. This provision is an attempt by the Democrats to prevent minority planks that address such divisive issues as abortion and homosexual rights from coming to the convention floor before millions of televiewers.

■ Unit rules permitting a majority of delegates from a state to cast the state's entire vote are still forbidden.

When the convention—Democratic or Republican—begins, the national chair soon yields the gavel to a temporary chair picked in advance by the national committee. He or she presides while housekeeping matters are taken care of and then yields to the permanent chair, who presides during the platform debates and the nominating activities. Instead of being elected by the convention, the permanent chair has come to be chosen ahead of the convention by consultation between the national chair and other party leaders, including presidential contenders. The convention merely ratifies the choice after it is presented. Since fairness to all contending factions by the presiding officer is a must if the convention is not to be disrupted, persons of stature and moderate temperament are chosen. Present and former speakers of the House of Representatives are especially favored.

The first highlight of the national convention is the famous "keynote address," usually give by the temporary chair. Even though this role is nine-tenths ritual, it is one that has launched more than one young regional leader with a stemwinding oratorical style on a national career.

The serious business of the convention begins with the acceptance of delegate credentials and convention rules. Despite reforms, credentials battles to determine who are bona fide delegates are likely to continue to flare up, for a nomination may hang in the balance. The national committee and the Credentials Committee try to iron out all disputes in advance, but the national convention has the final word, and floor fights over credentials are bound to occur. Victory for one faction may be a tip-off to the eventual nominee. A classic illustration of this took place at the Democrats' 1972 convention in what became known as the South Carolina/California delegation challenge. The question was whether McGovern could be stripped of the 271 delegates he had won in the California primary. To prevent this from happening, McGovern forces devised an ingenious parliamentary stratagem and successfully fended off the sabotage attempt by the Anybody But McGovern (ABM) movement, which was made up chiefly of Humphrey supporters.

If there are to be any fireworks at a convention, they will certainly appear when the Platform Committee presents its report. The significance of the platform does not lie in the fact that it will bind the nominees to a program. As noted earlier, those elected to office will interpret the platform to suit themselves. The platform is significant, first, because, like credentials, it may be an indication of who will be able to control the nomination. In the 1964 Republican convention, for example, conservatives controlled the Platform Committee and submitted a platform completely to the liking of Barry Goldwater, the conservative front-running contender. Liberal Republicans attempted to amend the platform on the floor but failed on practically every issue. From that point on, it was clear that Goldwater would be easily nominated. A platform may also serve a symbolic purpose, exposing discontents within a party and providing an occasion for debate that allows dissidents to vent their grievances. An outstanding illustration: The special time devoted to debate over the Vietnam War at the 1968 Democratic convention. The platform still reflected a fairly "hawkish" view of the war, but "doves" had been able to score a number of points. All in all, then, platform debate is far more than a useless activity.

Party platforms often speak very directly and firmly on settled issues or those on which the party has long had a stand. However, since party unity on issues is an important goal of platforms, they tend to be less specific, even ambiguous, on issues currently in conflict within the party or between the parties. A national convention has no power to bind its nominees or the nominees for Congress to specific courses of action. Once elected, the president (or congressional leadership for the out-party) beccmes the government and decides, as a practical matter, what the platform of the party is.

NOMINATING THE PRESIDENT

While debates over housekeeping matters and the platform are going on, delegations will caucus and recaucus, presidential hopefuls and those empowered to speak for them will try to build up their delegate strength, promises will be made and, perhaps, bargains struck.[3] With the final platform plank completed, attention will turn to the convention's chief purpose, the nomination of the president.

A candidate's name is placed in nomination by a prominent supporter during a roll call of the states. In past conventions, the states have been called alphabetically with top-of-the-alphabet states yielding to states prepared to nominate a front-running candidate. In 1972 the Democrats decided to determine the order of nomination by lot, and a Republican study group (the Delegates and Organizations Committee or the DO Committee) recommended this practice for Republicans, but the national committee did not accept it for 1976 or 1980.

After each candidate is nominated, there has traditionally been a demonstration of support from delegates plus a series of seconding speeches. This procedure has been something of a farce, with demonstrations far from spontaneous (participants have been hired in some cases) and much too long, and seconding speeches long-winded and repetitious.

The most notable difference between the two major party conventions in 1972, aside from the unconscionable length of some of the Democrats' sessions, was that—with the nomination locked up for Nixon—the GOP's was a huge media event replete with dress rehearsals, "multicolored trial balloons" coming out of plas-

---

[3]The candidates operate by phone or through representatives. It has traditionally been considered bad form for candidates to appear at the convention hall before nominations are made.

tic garbage bags, bands playing, stringent controls on who could be admitted to the convention floor, coordinated uniforms, and chants of "Four More Years."

To make the entire scene more businesslike (and—not incidentally—more appealing to a television audience), the Democrats since 1972 have been limiting to 15 minutes the total time for a candidate's nomination and seconding speeches, including any spontaneous demonstrations. Planned demonstrations have been banned. The Republican party has limited each nominating speech to 15 minutes, but has not prohibited planned demonstrations.

To further speed up the nominating process, both parties have looked at the problem of favorite sons. In 1976, the Democrats required that candidates establish substantial support in three or more states by a petition method before their names may be placed in nomination. For Republicans, only evidence of delegate support from three states is required to establish one as a serious candidate. Both parties, then, are attempting to streamline and take much of the sham out of conventions.

After all candidates' names have been placed in nomination, there is another roll call of states to determine the nominee. Here again, the conventions for many years proceeded alphabetically, beginning with Alabama. This meant that states later in the alphabet were always in a better position than earlier states to gain increased power and prestige by providing the votes that put a candidate over the top. In 1980 the order of the roll for the Democrats will be determined entirely by lot.

In addition, dilatory actions of the past, such as flowery speeches by the chair of a delegation when announcing the state's vote or the polling of each member of a delegation, will be discouraged. States may pass when their turn comes and vote at the end of the roll call or switch their votes before the final tally is announced. These measures are sometimes engaged in as tactical maneuvers or to get on the bandwagon for a winning candidate.

In both parties now, a majority vote is sufficient to nominate. If no candidate receives a majority on the first ballot, the roll is called again until someone does receive a majority. Previously, a majority of one in a delegation could swing the entire delegation's voting strength behind a particular candidate, but this is no longer permitted. In the Democratic party all but uncommitted delegates are bound for the first ballot to the candidate they were elected to support, unless released in writing by the candidate. In the Republican party, delegates must follow state law as to what ballot they are bound.

While the roll call of states edges along in a close ballot, millions of people all over the country mark convention tally sheets or follow the tallies of radio and television. When, finally, a state delegation's vote carries a candidate past the tip point to victory, pandemonium breaks loose in the convention hall. It is a difficult feat to finish calling the roll.

CHOOSING THE VICE-PRESIDENT

One more task faces the delegates before they can head for home, and that is to nominate a vice-presidential candidate. The official nomination, as in the case of the presidential candidate, is made by state roll call, but the procedure is less suspenseful in this instance. Traditionally, the wishes of the presidential nominee are honored in the choice of running mate. That choice is known to all by roll-call time so that the nomination is a formality only and is sometimes made by acclamation. Occasionally there is some grumbling from delegates and even (though seldom) a battle for the nomination, as in 1956 at the Democratic convention when presidential nominee Adlai Stevenson threw the vice-presidential nomination open to the convention.

Since the vice-presidency has long been considered an unimportant office, the selection of a nominee has usually been largely a matter of balancing the election ticket for maximum vote-getting potential. So it was that Democratic nominee John F. Kennedy had few qualms about picking the more conservative Lyndon Johnson as his running mate in 1960. And southerner Jimmy Carter, with similar reasoning, chose liberal Minnesota Senator Walter Mondale for his running mate in 1976.

The Constitution assigns the vice-president very few duties other than to succeed to the office of president if it becomes vacant or if the president becomes disabled and unable to function as president. But in recent years the office, which rarely got much attention in the past, has become a subject of controversy. Franklin Roosevelt's death during tenure, Eisenhower's serious illnesses, Kennedy's assassination, Nixon's resignation, and the inadvertent nomination of a vice-presidential candidate with a history of psychiatric treatment all have served to warn the nation that the individual chosen to fill the vice-president's role must be of presidential timber.

Critics in both parties question the present—and long-standing—process of vice-presidential selection, deploring the haste shown in choosing a president's running mate and the haphazard manner of doing so. Many also object to the fact that the victorious presidential nominee does the choosing, leaving delegates no role except to endorse, *pro forma*. Criticism does not end there. The role of the vice-president has been a nonrole, and some want to see that changed. At one end of the spectrum is Arthur Schlesinger, Jr., who has called for abolition of the office. At the other extreme are those who call for multiple vice-presidents to share the work of administering the executive branch.

Beyond the questions already noted is the fundamental one of whether voters have a fair chance to vote for or against an individual who may ultimately become president. Given the present setup, a vote in the ballot box for a presidential candidate is an automatic vote for the running mate. Voters who are vehemently opposed to the vice-presidential nominee have no way of voting against him or her, unless they decide to vote against the presidential nominee as well.

Both political parties have looked for methods of selecting vice-presidents that would be less haphazard, more democratic, and more workable. Among the proposals (none of which has been taken very seriously by either party):

■ Allow up to 30 days after the convention to choose the nominee, subject to mail ratification by the convention delegates after an independent investigation of the nominee's background.

■ Have each presidential candidate name one to six potential vice-presidential nominees two weeks before the party convention and allow the convention delegates to make the choice from the successful candidate's list within 24 hours after the presidential nomination.

■ Have the presidential nominee submit a list of acceptable running mates within two weeks after the convention, for later consideration by the delegates.

THE ACCEPTANCE SPEECH

The final big moment for the convention is the acceptance speech by the presidential nominee. This custom is comparatively new. Before 1936, delegations were sent to inform the candidates of their nominations, and they did not go to the conventions. In 1936, however, Franklin D. Roosevelt flew to Chicago to accept the nomination personally, and all candidates have done so since. The acceptance speech sets the tone for the coming election and is, in a sense, a campaign speech, although candidates usually do not begin formal campaigning until Labor Day. In 1964, when Goldwater, throwing down the gauntlet to those who had attempted to condemn "extremism" at the convention, proclaimed that "extremism in the defense of liberty is no vice," he was signaling that he did not intend to moderate his views during the coming campaign as conservative candidates had often done.

TELEVISION AT THE NATIONAL CONVENTIONS

Along with party reforms, radio and television have removed much of the secret, "smoke-filled room" atmosphere from the national conventions. Television, especially, with its live coverage of events in and around the convention hall and convention city, has brought the conventions into millions of homes. For many people, the most memorable aspects of the conventions have not been keynote speeches but the wry humor of David Brinkley, the bitter reporting of Walter Cronkite at the 1968 Democratic convention, or the vision of John Chancellor being arrested on the floor of the 1964 Republican convention.

So complete is television coverage that the activities of the media may overshadow the doings of the delegates themselves. In San Francisco in 1964, by one count, the Republican party issued 3,983 badges to representatives of broadcast journalism (editorial and technical) to report on the activities of only 2,616 party delegates and alternates.[4] To many critics, this is a case of the tail wagging the dog. They complain that the television networks often cut away from convention proceedings (such as seconding speeches) to present what is essentially their own material—interviews, specials, reports from hotels, and the like. In addition, there is the question of television bias. Charges of bias reached a new high at the Democratic convention in 1968 when NBC and CBS, both feeling that their reporters were being too roughly handled by convention authorities and Chicago police, openly criticized the way the convention was being run. Cronkite's remarks were especially caustic, leading to a few demands that the networks be restricted in the future to covering official convention proceedings.

All networks had prime-time coverage of the two conventions in 1976, but ABC broadcast only main events. In 1980, television reporters and their roving cameras may be restricted in their movements in the convention hall or possibly even banned from the floor entirely. Nonetheless, both parties take care to schedule their more important events at a time when television viewing is likely to be at its peak. It may be inconvenient for politicians to trip over TV cables and hide from cameras, but TV coverage adds up to a plus for the voter. The careful viewer is likely to know as much as or more than the delegates themselves about what is going on at the convention. Like the football watcher, the stay-at-home participant has the advantage of the instant replay and the behind-the-scenes interview. Undoubtedly, more Americans are aware of how a president is nominated than ever before, thanks to television.

---

[4]Robert MacNeil, *The People Machine,* p. 95.

7

Phase four: The campaign

By Labor Day of a presidential election year, both candidates and voters will be campaign-weary. The candidates will have been campaigning, in one way or another, for four years and will be nearly exhausted by recent efforts in primaries and state conventions. The voters will have been exposed to literally millions of bits of political information and exhortation. Yet both candidates and voters must gird themselves for the final effort, the real, toe-to-toe presidential campaign that extends from Labor Day to the Tuesday after the first Monday in November.

CAMPAIGN ORGANIZATION

The principal purpose of a presidential campaign is to woo voters by appealing to as many kinds of people as possible in as many different ways as possible. To do this with a potential electorate of more than 100 million people is a staggering task that demands good organization, adequate manpower, and large amounts of money. The day of the "front-porch campaign" is over. In 1860 Abraham Lincoln won the election for the Republican party without leaving Springfield, Illinois, or making a single speech. One hundred years later, Republican nominee Richard Nixon traveled 65,000 miles, made 212 speeches, visited all 50 states—and lost.

Since Eisenhower entered politics in 1952, presidential candidates have created temporary national organizations to elect themselves without the direct support of their national and state parties. These committees were made mandatory by the FECA— at any rate for handling campaign finances. The organizations have become increasingly professional yet at the same time have grown more reliant on outside consultants. These outsiders— political consultants, media experts, pollsters—give advice on where to target efforts, recommend tactics, highlight voter perceptions of candidates, and identify the candidate's strengths and weaknesses.

A modern presidential campaign is big business, but unlike a modern corporate enterprise it is not structured along neat bureaucratic lines. A presidential campaign, in the words of campaign finance specialist Herbert E. Alexander, is a "multimillion dollar operation run by an amazing assemblage of amateurs and professionals, family and friends, specialists, job seekers, old hands and new faces, party bureaucrats, statesmen, and hangers-on."[1]

There are essentially three organizational elements in a presidential campaign: the candidate's personal campaign committee, which is assembled during the preliminary and primary phases of the campaign; the regular party organization headed by the national committee; and the volunteer citizens' groups that spring up before and after the conventions. A large part of the success of a campaign depends upon how well the three elements are utilized. The organizations need not be meshed in any particular way, but one point is essential: The presidential nominee must have the final word on all matters, and the campaign manager chosen by the nominee, whether serving as national chairman or not, must be the boss of the campaign. Divided leadership usually means lack of leadership and electoral disaster.

Since the work of volunteer groups is nearly always separate from the other campaign organizations, the real organizational question concerns the relationship between the candidate's own operation and the national committee. The party can provide some funds, volunteer help, contacts, get-out-the-vote drives, opinion research, publicity, and other resources to individual

---

[1]"Financing the Parties and Campaigns," *The Presidential Election and Transition 1960–61* (Washington, D.C.: Brookings Institution, 1961), p. 126.

party candidates and can help garner support from special interest groups. In 1972 Nixon's personal campaign organization, the Committee to Re-Elect the President, popularly known as CREEP, was completely separate from the party. It was run by White House staffers, some of whom had never run for office or had any experience on other campaigns, while the Republican National Committee accepted a secondary role.

Volunteer groups in a presidential campaign are of two kinds. First are the party-affiliated groups such as Young Democrats or Republicans, State Federation of Republican or Democratic Women, and local or district Democratic or Republican clubs. They are organizationally separate from the parties but dovetail their work with the regular organization. A second type is the "Citizens for John Doe Club." Such groups spring to life in every presidential campaign and are kept organizationally distinct for several reasons. They provide a way for volunteers to work for the national ticket without working for all party candidates. They may also provide a special way to appeal to specific groups such as ethnic minorities. In 1960, for example, some 200 local-level Viva Kennedy clubs were organized in the 21 states with concentrations of Spanish-speaking citizens. Both parties also receive help in the form of money and volunteers from the major pressure groups such as labor, business, and agriculture. (See the section on campaign finance later in this chapter for a discussion of the type of assistance such groups may legally give.) No party can depend upon complete support from any interest group, however. Labor unions, for example, have long been a prime source of support for the Democratic party, but their efforts were divided in 1968 when many rank-and-file union members overrode their national leadership to work for George Wallace. People from the business community, often thought of as being pro-Republican, also make contributions to the Democrats.

CAMPAIGN STRATEGY

Campaign strategy is a plan for winning. A winning political campaign means efficient use of limited resources (time, money, and people), appeal to a broad constituency, and successful neutralization of criticism of candidate and issues. As earlier passages have indicated, the presidential nominees' strategy decisions have their beginnings long before the party prize is won, but they meet their real test in the months after the convention, and they have, at this stage, an altogether new context: one on one.

If ever there had been a formula handbook written on how to win, it would be at the publisher's right now, undergoing serious revision. The tides of change were already coming in, but after Watergate they turned into tidal waves. The party reforms previously discussed and the Federal Election Campaign Act (FECA) of 1971 as revised in 1974 and 1976 are two important new determinants. But the most important is the mood of the public, at once more apathetic and more guarded, its cynicism—never far from the surface—at what may be an all-time high.

The 1976 amendments to the FECA mean that the style of running for the presidency must change. There are now stiff limits on how much an individual may contribute to a candidate. No longer may a few friendly "fat cats" bankroll a candidate's entire campaign.

■ The availability of federal matching funds will have had its chief impact earlier on—possibly affecting the choice of nominee by encouraging numbers of hopefuls to hang on right up to convention time.

The proliferation of primaries in 1976 forced candidates to make some key decisions early in the game:

—*whether—and how soon—to announce.* In 1976, as in 1972, some candidates began as early as two years before the election year to build up name recognition, gain momentum, dig up financial support, and develop a campaign organization;

—*whether to go after a batch of primary victories;*

—*whether to run only in selected primaries* and, if so, which ones;

—*whether to wait* until the national party convention convened, hoping to emerge as a compromise candidate.

■ Republican and Democratic nominees who accept public funds during the general election campaign may not seek or accept private contributions.

The first major strategy decision a campaign organization must make is to determine exactly what sort of "pitch" is needed to win the election. Does the candidate want to score with charisma and charm in a popularity contest—or work on developing issues packages?

Many candidates are advised to blur their positions, avoid clear distinctions between themselves and their opponents, and rely on flashy rhetoric that creates a good image and can be interpreted in any of several ways by different people. If an issue is really hot and a candidate speaks out on one side of it, such forthrightness may inspire all those who disagree to active opposition.

Political writer Richard Reeves suggests that the most success-ful politician may be the candidate who creates no enemies—the lowest common denominator.[2] And Alex Armedaris, president of a campaign management firm, advises candidates to sound as if they are saying something but actually to say nothing. "A strong posi-tion on an issue will only turn some voters off."

But recently, especially since Watergate, reformers, a more aggressive press, and the voters themselves have appeared to demand that candidates take more definite stands on the issues. During the nominating process it is crucial for candidates to mobilize early support from a squadron of devoted workers and the small numbers of voters who turn out for primaries and cau-cuses. Thus, candidates are motivated to take strong stands in order to appeal to a dedicated group of zealous supporters in the initial stages of their campaigns. But they must be cautious enough to allow for flexibility later on, when they need to appeal to a broader electorate, without appearing to renege on earlier commitments.

Candidates are often urged to take note of the so-called McGovern fiasco and Goldwater debacle. Many agree that McGovern's failure to generate a broad coalition of strength early in the campaign would have resulted in doomsday later on, even without some of his ideas for tax and welfare reform or failures in judgment, which damaged his credibility and raised questions about his decisiveness. And Goldwater's denunciation of Social Security, which is said to have caused thousands of Republicans to cross party lines and support Johnson, is supposed to have been a

[2]Richard Reeves, *A Ford, Not a Lincoln.*

factor in his defeat.[3] Strategists must make the key decision of how the candidate is to be distinguished from the large number of other contenders without creating too many enemies. This means making specific choices about the kind of image to be projected, the issues to be emphasized, and the stands to be taken.

Another key strategy decision involves *timing*. Most campaign experts believe that a certain momentum should be developed in a campaign, beginning with a limited, low-key approach and building to a climax as election day draws near. Candidates have been advised by financial consultants to spend a fourth of their money during the first half of their campaign and three-fourths during the second half.

But how are strategies developed to begin with? Candidates rely heavily on experts—the professional campaign specialists. Among this latter group, pollsters are particularly important. The reason is simple: Public opinion polls play a crucial role in a candidate's decisions about postures to take, approaches to use, shadings to give to statements on the issues.

CAMPAIGN TACTICS

Once matters of overall strategy are decided, the presidential campaign must resolve questions of tactics—the specific things to be done to win votes. Here again, professional experts have moved in, shouldering aside the "pols" as well as the nominee's friends in determining what to do. Among the questions each campaign must consider are: What are the best ways to raise and spend limited money? Where should the candidate campaign the hardest? How should the candidate deal with the press? What role should women or minorities play in the campaign? How can volunteer support best be recruited and used? How should wives and families be used?

Raising money

Direct mail was first used in a big way to raise money by Goldwater in the 1964 campaign, and in 1972 both Nixon and McGovern took full advantage of it. By 1976, direct mail was

---

[3]See *Senior Power: A Political Action Handbook for Senior Citizens.*

recognized as a basic fundraising tool, and direct-mail specialists have become increasingly important for many candidates. While direct mail is relatively expensive and something of a gamble, it is well suited to the solicitation of the many small contributions called for under a major premise of the new campaign finance law (see below in the section on campaign finance reforms). With the large number of Republicans in the race in 1980, however, the risk of attempting to draw water too often from the same well is considerable.

The universally used **"boiler room"** method is canvassing by phone—dialing-for-dollars—to drum up financial support for a candidate. The name derives from the fact that the work is generally relegated to volunteer workers and lower-grade staff. But even top-level campaigners occasionally participate in this kind of drive.

Celebrity events, because of a quirk in the new finance law (see below), have become a major source of revenue for most candidates. Recruiting entertainers to perform in benefit concerts or athletes to play in starstudded tennis or golf tournaments has netted a lot of cash for candidates—as much as $75,000 from one event alone.

Telethons are used either as fundraising devices or as question-and-answer sessions directly between candidate and voter.

"Contact cats" are former "fat cat" contributors limited by the reform act to donations of $1,000 per candidate per election. They are approached now for their contacts with other wealthy potential supporters rather than for huge personal contributions.

Special interests can be a major source of campaign funds. While corporations and unions are prohibited by law from making direct political contributions, they may establish political action committees (PACs) to which individuals are free to make voluntary contributions. In addition, the committees perform many valuable services for the candidates they back: They mobilize workers to elect candidates and pay for computer operations, phone-banks, printing, mailing and sound equipment. They also contact members and sponsor "nonpartisan" registration and get-out-the-vote campaigns.

Testimonial dinners, cocktail parties, teas, and other gatherings can be used to raise money as well as to recruit volunteers.

A candidate's personal funds, briefly restricted by the 1974 finance reform amendments, are now back in the picture. Early in 1976, the Supreme Court struck down the law's across-the-board curbs on using personal funds.

Spending money

Newspaper ads are traditional. Some candidates or groups supporting a candidate buy space in local or national newspapers and periodicals to promote the candidate.

Television/radio spots are by far the most costly of all the items in a campaign budget, though there has been a leveling off of spending lately: In 1968 presidential campaigners spent $14.6 million on television and $5.7 million on radio; in 1972 they spent less than half that amount. (See also the section in this chapter on the use of TV and radio by candidates.)

Direct mail requires an extensive "front end" outlay to get both money and votes. Direct-mail specialists help candidates determine formats and techniques that will make the effort worthwhile. Donor lists comprising religious, political, cultural, civic, welfare, educational, health, and international groups are those most often tapped. Also used are the various lists of such groups as periodicals subscribers, mail-order buyers, licensed drivers, registered voters, wealthy persons, women, senior citizens, and families with children. Toward the end of the campaign more specialized lists are used to make pinpointed appeals for votes.

Leafleting is a tried-and-true campaign technique. Posters, pamphlets, and flyers publicize candidate positions and campaign issues; give voters information on registration procedures, dates of election, or location of campaign headquarters; solicit funds and/or volunteer help.

Media events seek to capture press coverage by gearing campaigning to the visual—coffee klatch appearances, visits by family and supporters to rest homes and hospitals, rides in motorcades, attendance at fairs and other crowd-gathering events. The days of baby kissing are not entirely gone, nor will they be so long as such hoopla gets free media attention. But arranging it all costs money.

Travel is a *must*. Candidates and their staffs spend a lot of time on the road, using airplanes, automobiles, trains, and buses. Often volunteers are sent to remote rural areas to organize supporters and set up campaign organizations.

Telephone expenses can run into thousands of dollars for calls to regional, local, and statewide campaign organizations, to the press, party leaders, and others, and for making get-out-the-vote drives, taking surveys, etc.

Polls are expensive, but candidates all feel the need for them: to take the voter's pulse, to measure the impact of a campaign, or to determine voters' concerns. A poll showing that a candidate has more popular support than expected can boost the prospects of a relatively unknown candidate.

Staffing doesn't come cheap. Though most candidates have relatively few paid staffers, professional bigwigs cost money, and even unpaid volunteers are reimbursed for much of their travel and organizational expenses.

Consultants—media and political experts—are increasingly being used, and accountants and lawyers are needed to help campaign staffs understand and comply with the new finance law.

Allocating resources

There are literally thousands of choices to be made about what to do when—and where to do it. Candidates who derive their greatest strength from certain labor or ethnic groups may well channel more of their resources in those directions than in wooing hostile groups. Some candidates rely mainly on personal appearances, while others, such as Wallace in 1976, make heavy use of the media to reach voters. Deciding which states should get extra effort and when is an arcane art in itself. Much depends on the importance of a state, either because of its electoral vote strength or because of the prominent political figures and groups to be courted there that may sway large blocs of voters. On election day the get-out-the-vote effort can be crucial. Potential supporters are urged by telephone or door-to-door canvassers to go to the polls. Handicapped voters and senior citizens are offered rides to the voting booths.

Political consultants play a key role in deciding how limited time, staff, and other resources should best be used. And almost every candidate's campaign resources are limited. The decision may boil down to whether the candidate is going to be spread too thin or oversaturate an area that is either immovably hostile or already safe turf. Computers are increasingly used to determine voting patterns, to learn what the constituency is and what support can be expected and, right before the conventions, to analyze and monitor delegates one by one.

Volunteers are the lifeblood of any campaign, and volunteer senior citizens often play a vital role. Their years of experience can help because of their long-term community contact and their proven skills as local fundraisers. Other volunteer chores range from babysitting and helping in voter registration to field organization and press contacts.

Making a new place for women

The year 1972 was a turning point for women in political campaigns, especially in the process of "choosing the president." Jean Westwood was appointed head of the Democratic National Committee, the first woman to serve in this capacity. In 1974 Mary Louise Smith became chair of the Republican National Committee. But of more far-reaching importance has been the broad acceptance of women in positions formerly reserved to men. In 1976 some candidates made a bow to the enhanced place of women in politics by establishing "women's affairs divisions" to address issues affecting women—abortion, day-care centers, equal employment. But other candidates went further by appointing women to key positions on their campaign staffs. In 1976 two women served as deputy managers and several others served as press and scheduling secretaries rather than in the clerical or volunteer positions they might once have been relegated to. From token party roles women are speedily moving into positions in which they share in strategy decisions and play an equal part in formulating tactics.

There is obviously still a distance for women to go before they attain parity with men in presidential politics. Early in 1976, Ellen McCormack, running under a "right to life" anti-abortion banner, as a candidate for the Democratic nomination, qualified for federal matching funds. To date there are no serious women contenders for the 1980 nomination in either major party.

Wives and daughters of presidential candidates have always participated in political campaigns. In the past, however, their role was superficial, and rarely would they express opinions that deviated from those of their husbands or fathers. A notable exception was Franklin D. Roosevelt's wife, Eleanor, who energetically campaigned for her husband and helped formulate campaign strategy. Recently, the situation has begun to change. In 1972 Eleanor McGovern actively served as part of her husband's team, going out on a speaking circuit of her own. In 1976 several wives in both parties waved their own banners. Betty Ford created a stir when she lobbied for the Equal Rights Amendment just before the 1976 campaign started. In late 1979, Carter was relying on the campaign skills of his wife, Rosalynn.

The question of how to deploy families and wives is always a tactical matter, dependent on their enthusiasm and ability to speak well. It changes from campaign to campaign.

CAMPAIGN FINANCE

In 1860 the Republican party spent $100,000 to elect Lincoln president; 100 years later that sum bought only 30 minutes of network television time.[4] Twelve years later, $62 million was spent for Nixon to win and $30 million for McGovern to lose. The price of campaigning has skyrocketed because of inflation, the expanding constituency, the enormous costs of television and radio time, the wide use of air travel, and reliance on high-priced computers and consultants.

Despite much tongue-clucking about the evils of high-spending electoral politics and a few inept efforts over the years to legislate morality in campaign finance, the costs (and the methods of meeting them) were accepted with resignation by candidates, government, and public. It took a Watergate to galvanize Congress into establishing some tough controls on financing of presidential elections as well as Senate and House races. In an effort to cleanse American politics of the kind of financial corruption the Watergate scandals exposed, the Federal Election Campaign Act (FECA) Amendments of 1974 were enacted. Their basic premise was that

---

[4]Hugh Bone, *American Politics and the Party System*, p. 91.

it is ethically wrong for wealthy contributors to bankroll elections and that nothing short of major change could reform the process.

The day after its passage, the law was challenged in the courts by an unlikely alliance of reformers: independent presidential candidate Eugene McCarthy, Conservative-Republican Senator James Buckley, and Stewart Mott, General Motors heir and political philanthropist.

The Supreme Court's January 1976 ruling upheld most of the law's provisions. But it struck down some key provisions with the result that in the heat of the 1976 campaign Congress had to enact a new set of amendments to the FECA. After Supreme Court surgery and congressional patchwork, this is what the campaign finance reforms look like:

Disclosure

■ Rigorous reporting of all campaign expenditures and contributions is required. Candidates must form a political committee that reports all contributions and expenditures over $100, identifying the donor's name, mailing address, and place of business.

Spending

■ Presidential aspirants may spend no more than a total of $30 million —$10 million on the nomination process, $20 million during the general election[5]—if they wish to get federal matching funds. If they do not accept federal money, however, there is no limit.

Federal funds[6]

■ To qualify for federal matching funds in their primary campaigns, presidential candidates must raise at least $5,000 in each of 20 states in contributions of $250 or less. During the nomination process, contributions of $250 or less are then matched, up to a total of $5 million.

---

[5]Candidates are allowed another 20 percent for fundraising costs, and adjustments are made for annual inflationary increases.
[6]The money for all this federal funding comes from a kitty made up of the money citizens may earmark on their income tax returns; each taxpayer may check off one tax dollar for this purpose.

- Major party nominees are automatically entitled to $20 million in the postconvention campaign period, with no matching requirement, for qualified campaign expenses.
- Minor party candidates qualifying for funds do not get their money until after the election, and then in an amount proportionate to the popular votes they received.
- Each major party convention gets $2 million from the government.

Contributions

- Individual contributors are limited to giving $1,000 to any one candidate during one election, although the nomination process is treated as a separate election. Donors may give a combined total of up to $25,000 to all federal election campaigns held during the same year. This limitation does not include the value of time volunteered by an individual; nor does it include up to $500 worth of food, beverage, or space donated to a candidate, or up to $500 in unreimbursed travel expenses.
- Although direct contributions to candidates are limited, the Supreme Court ruled that there are no limits on how much individuals and groups may spend for "independent expenditures" on behalf of a candidate, so long as the money is spent independently and not coordinated with the candidate. Stewart Mott, the "fat cat" litigant, says the decision puts him back in business and that he might spend up to $100,000 on presidential races, since he could apply his money to "independent projects."
- Multicandidate political committees may contribute no more than $5,000 per candidate per election.
- Direct spending by national parties in behalf of presidential candidates is limited to 2 cents per person of voting age.
- Candidates who accept federal funds are limited to using $50,000 of personal and family funds.

Enforcement

- The Federal Election Commission (FEC), created by the 1974 act and reconstituted by the 1976 amendments, polices the FECA.

The FEC has a difficult job administering a complex law. Many people are disappointed at what they see as loopholes in the FECA. They point to such escape clauses as these:

- Corporations and unions may spend unlimited amounts for

election activities directed at their own stockholders and members, respectively. Corporate and union funds may also be used to establish *political action committees* that are vehicles for stockholders, employees, or members to make voluntary contributions. These committees may then make limited contributions to candidates.

■ Incumbents retain their present advantages of office inasmuch as they are still in a position to stretch the use of office funds and franking privileges.

■ Rich candidates might have an advantage, because they may spend unlimited amounts of their own money, if they decline federal funds.

Continuing objections

Loopholes and enforcement weaknesses aside, opponents of a strong federal role in campaign finance continue to raise philosophical and pragmatic objections, such as these:

■ Contribution limits abridge First Amendment rights because they arbitrarily control citizen expression of support for candidates.

■ Disclosure requirements abridge the right to free speech and free association guaranteed by the First Amendment because of the possibility of harassment of contributors to unpopular causes.

■ Public financing favors the major political parties.

■ Candidates lose control of their own campaigns, since independent, uncoordinated expenditures by others on their behalf is unlimited.

■ Low contribution limits hinder relatively unknown or poor candidates and those who start late, since essential "seed money" cannot be solicited from a few big donors.

■ Once initial payments have been made to major parties, there may not be enough money left in the federal matching funds kitty for those running on third-party tickets.

■ The need to maintain elaborate bookkeeping and expenditure records costs candidates a lot of time and money, and there is also the danger of discouraging volunteers, who might be afraid of inadvertently violating the complex law.

■ The law affects the role of political parties. No longer will they play a pivotal role in presidential campaign fundraising, since they are limited in the amount they may spend on behalf of a candidate. They will be relegated to providing backup services, such as running informational seminars for candidates, developing mailing lists of party contacts, sponsoring polls, organizing volunteers and voter registration drives, and promoting general support for the party slate as a whole.

Impact on the 1976 presidential race

Only one federal election has been held since the FECA was amended in 1976. While political scientists warn against conclusions based on only one experience, it is possible to observe some differences between 1976 and preceding elections.

The availability of public funds lessened the burden of raising funds for candidates and parties in three ways:

■ A total of $24.6 million in matching funds was made available to 15 qualified candidates of the 100 who applied. Each candidate could have received up to $5.45 million. Democrats received 60 percent of all matching funds, reflecting the larger number of primary candidates in their party.

■ It was not necessary for parties to seek funding for nominating conventions. The FECA provides up to $2.18 million for conventions; in 1976 $2.01 million went to the Democrats and $1.5 million to the Republicans for their nominating conventions. This compares with 1972 figures of $1.7 million for the Democrats and $1.9 million for the Republicans, all raised by private donations.

■ Jimmy Carter and Gerald Ford each received $21.8 million in public funds for their general election campaigns, in exchange for which they gave up the right (and the burden) of seeking private contributions—a striking change from the 1972 election campaign, which has become notorious for the number of illegal corporate donations and for the large sums contributed by individual donors.

As a result of the FECA, the $43.6 million total expenditure for the 1976 presidential election was substantially lower than that for the 1972 McGovern and Nixon campaigns, which spent $30 million and $60 million, respectively. One result of the smaller sums available for campaigning was that both the Ford and Carter campaigns spent a large proportion of their budgets on mass-media advertising in order to gain as much impact from their dollars as they could.

The FECA has received high marks for curbing the questionable campaign practices evident in the 1972 presidential election and for providing the opportunity for little-known candidates to compete effectively. However, some analysts blame tight budgeting for the decrease of campaign activity, lower campaign exposure, and the increase in public apathy that together produced lower voter turn-out in the 1976 election.

MASS MEDIA IN CAMPAIGNING

Although some voters learn about candidates through direct mail, word of mouth, or leaflets left at their door, most information on presidential candidates comes through the mass media—television, radio, newspapers, and magazines. This means that the way the media cover the campaign and the way the candidates buy and use paid media advertising can make all the difference in how the election comes out.

News media coverage

For the national news media, covering a presidential campaign has taken on the proportions of conducting a major military campaign. The logistics alone present a significant organizational challenge. Together, the three major networks sent several hundred reporters, camera people, technicians, and backup crew to cover the 1976 New Hampshire primary. Carrying stories about a campaign as much as two years before it begins has become standard procedure. Today's media have the ability to determine the shape and substance of a campaign—the ability to mold images, to define issues, to play up some candidates and play down others, to interpret polls and the results of primaries, to generate a sense of gathering momentum or impending defeat. The power of the central corps of full-time national political correspondents, numbering no more than about 30, virtually all male, stems from their ability to influence opinion leaders and indirectly to affect which candidates are funneled money and support. Contributions are often determined by standings in media-highlighted polls, by image-making editorials, and by front-page headlines.

Given this potential power, journalists must make some key decisions—how much coverage should each candidate receive?

Should coverage focus on what the candidates say in official position papers, on the details of what they actually do in a day of campaigning, on their records in office? Or should an attempt be made to make analytical interpretations of their views and personalities?

Campaign reporting has gone through several different stages. Until 1960, campaign coverage was generally dry, to-the-point, and objective. It didn't excite the mass of American readers. Rather than risk injecting personal judgment into their writing, reporters wrote "formula" stories, as they're known in the trade, presenting information that didn't stray far from candidates' press releases.

But Theodore White changed political reporting with his chronicle of the Kennedy/Nixon race in the now-classic *Making of the President 1960*. Other journalists were embarrassed, because for the first time someone had laid out what a political campaign was all about—excitement and drama wrapped around good and bad guys who were scrambling for the "grand prize."

Since 1964, the name of the game has been the "Teddy White syndrome," action-packed, detail-crammed, everything-thrown-in coverage of presidential contenders. How a candidate parts his hair, the love life of his children—all has been fair game. Broadcast and print executives have felt that if they just had enough reporters on hand there would be no way an important story could slip by.

But some within the industry have begun to say that the overemphasis on mechanics and day-by-day trivia has been at the expense of examining such serious matters as where the candidates stand on issues and what their qualifications for office are. In one major newsgathering organization after another, there have been noises made about "rethinking campaign coverage" and questions raised about "Are we stressing style over substance?" And reporters have been showing more interest in candidates' ideas than in their tastes in food.[7]

---

[7]Even Theodore White himself, according to Timothy Crouse, said: "Who gives a _____ if the guy had milk and Total for breakfast?" In an interview, White also told Crouse that he sometimes feels as if he had created a Frankenstein's monster with his new methods of campaign reporting. For a revealing perspective on campaign press coverage, see Crouse's book on the 1972 campaign, *The Boys on the Bus*.

In the past, when candidates refused to be pinned down on their views, reporters would not push them. In 1972, for example, no reporter ever got Nixon to talk specifically about how he planned to get out of Vietnam. James Lehrer, correspondent for the National Public Affairs Center for Television (NPACT), has noted that candidates manipulate the press by avoiding questions they don't wish to address. "We condition people not to expect the truth in campaign coverage," says Lehrer. "How candidates handle the question becomes more important than whether they actually answer it."

But in the 1976 campaign, at least some journalists went after the substance. "You sound like a politician," Lawrence Spivak, longtime moderator of TV's *Meet the Press,* rebuked Senator Lloyd Bentsen, then a presidential candidate, when as a guest on the show early in the 1976 campaign Bentsen talked around a direct question.

Journalists also seem to be striving to present fewer of the simple, superficial type of stories and more of the probing, interpretive kind. Straight reporting of candidates' speeches—or pickups from press releases—give voters little help in figuring out whether the candidates' positions have depth or are workable.

An unprecedented number of columns, news programs, debates, forums, and editorials are stressing issues as never before. In the wake of Watergate, the health and finances of presidential contenders get full media treatment. More thought is given to the difficult-to-assess element of character and personality, and candidates are being rated on their candor, personal style, humor, and intelligence.

Of all the media, television bears the greatest responsibilities in campaign coverage, for it is the major source of political news for most voters, with 65 percent of the electorate gaining most of its knowledge of national candidates from it. Yet there are many obstacles to thorough television coverage of campaign issues. The medium thrives on visual events. Straightforward discussion of issues doesn't produce much color or excitement for TV cameras. And, until recently, the equal-time rules (see below) encouraged covering the showy "news" event rather than the dispassionate candidate debate. In 1972, for example, New York City's mayor, John V. Lindsay, attempting a run for the presidency, was filmed milking a cow just before the Wisconsin primary. The short time available for the evening news restricts any real analysis of issues, and TV costs play a large part in curbing ideal coverage. A two-minute news story, for instance, runs into four figures, while a 30-minute show can go as high as six figures.

But the networks are trying. News shows have devoted more time to candidate profiles, although critics complain that they still tend to be superficial. Early in 1976, the regular forums—*Meet the Press, Face the Nation,* and *Issues and Answers*—all induced the announced candidates to participate in grueling interview sessions, even if it had to be done in split sessions because of the large number of contenders. The Public Broadcasting System, the so-called Fourth Network, because it is noncommercial, can afford to take more time producing analytical profiles and nonpartisan, issue-oriented programs.

In 1976, a series of televised forums, in which voters and experts questioned the major presidential candidates, was sponsored by the League of Women Voters Education Fund in cooperation with PBS. The forums were planned to be held just prior to the major primaries and provided for in-depth consideration of one major issue area for each program. And after the party conventions, the LWVEF sponsored four debates—three between Ford and Carter and one between vice-presidential candidates Walter Mondale and Robert Dole—which were covered by the networks as a news event (see "Equal-time provisions" below). To sharpen the discussion, experienced reporters and issue experts quizzed the candidates.

While television is far superior to print in its ability to capture a large audience, the networks would be lost without the wire services, daily newspapers, and news weeklies. The print media can probe the personalities of candidates and offer extensive serialized treatises on every aspect of a campaign in a way television and radio are not equipped to do. Not being subject to the technical constraints of the broadcast trade and having less stringent deadlines to meet on both a daily and a long-term basis, journalists in the print media have much greater opportunity to fully develop coverage, no matter how many candidates are out on the campaign trail.

The national wire services—Associated Press (AP) and United

Press International (UPI)—provide the most widely circulated stories in the country. And what the wire reporters view as the "lead" of a story will often end up as the meat of the story in a thousand daily newspapers across the country. Because of tight deadlines and space limitations, however, these stories are generally not as analytical in nature as the syndicated by-line articles sent out by the *Los Angeles Times, Washington Post,* and *New York Times.*

One admitted shortcoming of all the media is their overreliance on polls, which can mislead by lagging behind the changing mood of the country, by taking a faulty sample, or by being just plain inaccurate. Before the primary season began in the 1972 campaign, an early Gallup poll showing Muskie as the favorite Democratic candidate for president caused reporters to expect him to gain a major victory in New Hampshire. They then called him a loser when he won a 47-percent plurality of the vote.

No one really knows the impact of the media's misinterpretations of polls and primary results on a presidential candidate's future. One candidate might be knocked right out of the race; another might get off and running with a lead.

Equal-time provisions

The so-called equal-time rule (Section 315) of the Federal Communications Act requires a broadcaster who sells or gives time to a candidate to make available equal opportunities to all competing candidates, including minor-party and independent candidates. In the past, this rule has effectively limited some coverage of major candidates by broadcasters who want to avoid opening up their air time to scores of minor candidates. The only exceptions to the rule occur when a candidate is shown in a bona fide newscast, interview or news documentary (where the candidate's appearance is only incidental to the subject of the documentary), or in on-the-spot coverage of a bona fide news event. Recently, the Federal Communications Commission ruled that such exempt news events may include debates and forums, so long as the event is sponsored by someone other than the broadcaster or the candidate. The LWVEF-sponsored Presidential Forums and Debates were broadcast under the newscast exemption.

Use of radio and TV by candidates

Candidates have come to rely extensively on the broadcast media to appeal for votes. Through short TV and radio spots or elaborately prepared TV feature programs produced by their own media specialists and lasting 15 minutes to an hour, candidates hope to accentuate their own qualities and downgrade their opponents'. Spot commercials are useful in projecting a vivid, dynamic image and are not usually intended to convey much information, though they sometimes deal with issues.

The importance of the mass media—particularly radio and television—is that they give quick, massive, national exposure. Expensive though that exposure be, it takes less energy than in-person appearances, makes it possible to use travel time more efficiently, and opens up a much wider audience. Personal contact may be more effective, but that becomes impractical when there's a whole nation to reach in a short time.

Use of television or radio spots peaks at the height of the campaign, usually just prior to election time. Many thoughtful persons fear that campaigns have become battles between advertising agencies rather than tests of candidates and issues. If much of a presidential campaign is stage-managed, they argue, voters will never see the "real" candidate or hear discussion of the "real" issues. They will be led Pied Piper fashion to support the slickest electronic candidate, regardless of the shallowness of his or her appeal.

The danger of television campaigning assumes frightening proportions to some critics when seen in the light of computer technology. Television commercials of whatever sort are increasingly based on survey research. Voters are polled as to what issues trouble them, what their attitudes are on certain issues, and how they respond to candidates. This material is then used to design a campaign that will appeal to voters' special interests or even exploit their fears. Some forward-looking politicians have even recommended the development of a kind of "people machine," a giant computer that would store all information gathered from such sources as opinion surveys and election statistics, then produce advice at the press of a button.[8] When this stage is reached,

---

[8]MacNeil, *The People Machine*, pp. 219–221.

say the critics, American politicians will no longer be leading but simply responding to the prejudices of a computerized electorate.

Media specialists defend their work on a number of grounds. They contend, on the one hand, that television is overrated, that it is only one campaign tool. On the other hand, they say that even if it is influential, political advertising serves the same purpose as commercial advertising—to inform viewers of the products available. And even short spots can be produced in such a way that they give straightforward information on a candidate's position. Viewers know that the information is biased in favor of the product and make the necessary adjustments in their thinking. Skeptics doubt this rationale, feeling that voters do not have enough defenses against the soft-sell and that, in any case, the media specialists are busily trying to stay ahead of whatever defenses viewers have. Occasionally, the professionals are candid about the business they're in. Says one media specialist: "Damned right we don't explain. We don't educate, we motivate. That's our job. We're not teachers, we're political managers. We're trying to win."

8
Phase five: The election

THE ELECTORAL COLLEGE SYSTEM

Who would imagine that the method by which the president and the vice-president of the United States are elected would be considered a complicated and inequitable mechanism perpetually in danger of breaking down? One reason for its rickety condition is that it is one of the less fine-tuned of the many compromises written into the Constitution in 1787. As usual, the founding fathers were trying for a balance between the states' and the people's interests. They never pictured the emergence of national political parties or a communications network able to bring two or three candidates before the entire electorate.

One of their hedges against "popular passion" was to provide that the president be chosen indirectly through the "electoral college" rather than directly by the voters in November. In the beginning, the electors had very real powers to work their will. Now, their sole function is to confirm a decision made by the electorate six weeks earlier.[1]

Under the Constitution, each state is authorized to choose electors for president and vice-president, the number always being the same as the combined number of U.S. senators and representatives allotted to the state. With 100 senators and 435 representa-

---

[1] An "elector" is simply a person who elects someone else. The term *college* refers to a decision-making group such as the College of Cardinals, which elects the pope.

tives in the United States, plus three electors for the District of Columbia provided by the Twenty-third Amendment, the total electoral college vote is 538.[2]

Makeup and operation of the electoral college itself is tightly defined by the Constitution, but the method of choosing electors is left to the states. In the beginning many states did not provide for popular election of the presidential electors. Today, however, electors are chosen by direct popular vote in every state—another illustration of the general trend toward democratizing the election process.

With the political parties in control of presidential politics, the function of the electoral college has changed drastically. Rather than having individuals seek to become electors and then vote for whomever they please for president, the parties have turned the process upside down by arranging slates of electors, all pledged to support the candidate nominated by the party.

In the earliest days of the electoral college, quite the opposite was true. Electors cast their votes for individual candidates rather than for party slates, with the majority winner being elected president and the runner-up, vice-president. This made for some bizarre situations, as in 1796 when the Federalist John Adams, with 71 votes, became president and the Democratic-Republican Thomas Jefferson, with 68, vice-president—roughly equivalent in modern times to an election in which Nixon and McGovern ended up as president and vice-president. Then in 1800 Jefferson and his running mate, Aaron Burr, each won an identical number of electoral votes, forcing the election into the House of Representatives, which resolved it in Jefferson's favor. It was to avoid any similar occurrence that the Twelfth Amendment was passed in 1804. This required the electors to cast two separate ballots, one for president and the other for vice-president. It has been the only constitutional change made in the electoral college system.

In over half the states, it is the names of the candidates rather

---

[2]For comprehensive discussions of the development and operation of the electoral college system—its pros and cons and possible reforms—see League of Women Voters of the United States, *Who Should Elect the President?*; Joseph Gorman, *Elections: Electoral College Reform*; and Lawrence D. Longley, "The Electoral College" in the "American Political Reform" issue of *Current History*, August 1974.

than the names of the electors that appear on the ballot; in the other states, both candidates and electors are identified. The victor in each state is determined by counting the votes for each slate of electors; the slate receiving the most votes, whether or not it is a majority of the votes cast, is declared elected.

To be elected to the presidency a candidate must receive an absolute majority (270) of the electoral votes cast. If no candidate receives a majority, the House of Representatives picks the winner from the top three, each state delegation in the House casting only one vote, regardless of its size. Only two American elections have been decided this way.

The vice-president is elected by the same indirect, winner-take-all method that chooses the president, but the electors vote separately for the two offices. If no vice-presidential candidate receives a majority, the Senate picks the winner from the top two, each senator voting as an individual. The Senate has not made the choice since 1836.

The electoral college pro and con

The electoral college mechanism has not lacked for critics over the years. The basic objection is that the system clearly has the potential to frustrate the popular will in the selection of a president and a vice-president. A candidate might not be elected even though he receives more popular votes than his opponent, possibly even a majority. This happened in 1824 (when the election was thrown into the House), in 1876 (when there were disputed electors from several states), and in 1888. The winner-take-all system means that millions of votes in every presidential election are cast for a candidate who, failing to carry a particular state, receives not a single *electoral* vote in that state for his *popular* votes. A minority, even a large one, becomes in effect no minority at all.

Another problem cited by critics is the possibility of "faithless electors" who defect from the candidate they are pledged to vote for. Most recently, in 1972 a Republican elector of Virginia deserted Nixon to vote for the Libertarian party candidate. Earlier, in 1968, Nixon had lost another Virginia elector, who bolted over to support George Wallace.

The primary danger of "faithless electors" is that the candidate who wins the popular vote could wind up one or two votes short of a majority in the electoral college and could lose the election on a technicality. This prospect becomes more probable when there are third-party candidates who could negotiate with electors before they vote.

Many see the apportionment system of the electoral college as a basic flaw, because it gives each of the smaller states "control" of at least three electoral votes, even though on a straight population basis some might be entitled to only one or two. This argument is sometimes extended to include ideological, geographical, and partisan bias—all of which are called undemocratic and unfair.

Critics of the system argue that the possibility of an election's being thrown into the House of Representatives is hardly comforting either, since for such a decision each state has a single vote, a fact which moves the choice even farther from democratic control. The two occasions when it occurred (1800 and 1824) were marked by charges of "deals" and "corrupt" bargains. In any event, giving each state one vote regardless of the population it represents is hardly recognition of one-person-one-vote (nor does it truly represent even the choice of the states in their individual corporate capacities). And, since the Senate chooses the vice-president under these circumstances, it is possible for the country to be confronted with a president and a vice-president of different parties. All in all, the critics see grave dangers inherent in the electoral college system.

Those who argue in favor of retaining the present system feel there is too much uncertainty over whether any other method would be an improvement. They point out that many of the complaints about the electoral college apply just as well to the Senate and, to some extent, the House. They worry about where the dismantling of the federal system would stop.

The second argument made by defenders of the electoral college is that the present method serves American democracy well by supporting the two-party system and thwarting the rise of the splinter parties that have plagued many European democracies. The winner-take-all system means that minor parties get few electoral votes and that a president who is the choice of the nation as a whole emerges. Nor do splinter groups find it easy to throw an election into the House. Other circumstances, not minor parties, were responsible for the two occasions when this occurred. Supporters feel strongly that if the electors fail to agree on a majority president, it is in keeping with the federal system that the House of Representatives, *voting as states,* makes the selection.

The third argument asserts that the electoral college system is a rare bird among the institutions passed down from an eighteenth-century agrarian society: It gives urban areas some leverage. In the many states where urban political power still tends to be minimized in state legislatures, urban votes carry clout under the winner-take-all electoral college system.

Proposals for change

Discontent has been stimulated in recent years by the Wallace third-party movement as well as by the Supreme Court one-person-one-vote ruling on legislative districting. A number of proposals for changing the way the president and the vice-president are elected have been made. Most would require a constitutional amendment, though states can change their state laws governing the way they choose electors.

One set of proposals looks toward keeping the electoral vote system but eliminating its winner-take-all features. This shift could be brought about by choosing most electors on a congressional district basis, with only two electors per state chosen statewide. A 1969 Maine law provides for this method, and legislation has been considered in several other states. Alternatively, electors (as people) could be eliminated and the electoral votes of a state simply assigned to candidates on the basis of the popular vote they received. Constitutional amendments to that effect have been introduced in Congress but none has passed. These changes might eliminate some distortion of the popular vote, but they would not answer the complaint that the people do not elect the president directly.

Senator Birch Bayh has repeatedly introduced a constitutional amendment providing for direct election of the president and the vice-president. Under the Bayh plan, candidates for president and vice-president would be required to run together in each state and the District of Columbia, and voters would make their choices directly, without any intervening slate of electors. If any pair of candidates received 40 percent of the nationwide popular vote, that pair would be declared elected; if no pair received that amount, there would be a runoff election between the two top pairs.

Direct election of the president along the lines of the Bayh plan would effectively bring the one-person-one-vote principle to presidential elections. In addition, according to its defenders, direct election would help the two-party system and encourage broader citizen participation by making every vote count. Any dangers to the federal system, they argue, would be more than outweighed by the right of all the people of the United States to choose their two top elected officials directly. Opponents of direct election hold that this particular plan for change might necessitate the holding of two elections because of the runoff provision, thus making the presidential election process even more costly and drawn out than it already is.

Much of the impetus for reform of the electoral college is dead, at least temporarily, after the defeat of the amendment on the Senate floor in the summer of 1979. Political observers speculate that the makeup of the 97th Congress will be a key factor in determining whether there will be any reform in the near future.

Election Day

A presidential election day is the consummation of the study, the planning and training, the grueling work and travel, the meeting and talking, the writing and speechmaking, the persuading and financing, that have been done on behalf of and by the presidential candidates. It is their day of victory or of defeat.

For many hundreds of other people, it is a long, hard day that starts for some at five in the morning when precinct workers, organized to catch voters before they leave for work, nail VOTE signs along the streets and slip reminder sheets under the doors of "their voters." In some places, the polls open at 6 A.M., and a full complement of poll workers, officials, watchers, policemen must be on hand. Dozens of kinds of tasks, painstakingly planned, have been assigned to volunteers and regular party workers of all ages and talents. Party poll watchers, message runners, drivers to take voters to the polls, teenagers to electioneer, all ages to babysit, housebound mothers to telephone registered voters who have not appeared at the polls, Scouts to give out "I have voted" tags—all swing into action for a long, tiring, exciting day.

Voting is supervised by election judges representing both parties. These officials are paid a fee, usually a nominal one. Their work begins before the polls open and is far from over when the polls close. They are responsible for proper voting procedure, whether paper ballots or voting machines are used, and for the conduct of the polling places. They may cast the absentee ballots and help those whose physical disabilities entitle them to assistance in the voting booth. They count the votes and report the official returns.

For the candidates, election day is like an opening night for a Broadway producer. Everything that can be done has been done or is being done by campaign workers. By tradition, candidates do not campaign on election day or even make public appearances other than to vote at their own polling places. As the day ends and the time for the polls to close approaches, each candidate, like millions of other Americans, settles in front of the television set and waits for the election results to come in.

REPORTING THE RESULTS

At one time, election nights in America were important social events. Friends and neighbors gathered at the local store or in private homes and entertained each other with food, drink, and conversation as the election results trickled in over telegraph wire or radio station. Spokesmen for candidates who were trailing in the early returns talked bravely of trends that had not yet developed and reminded supporters to "wait for the downstate returns." The leading candidates said cautiously that it was "too early to tell yet" and continued to make gloomy predictions until it was time to claim victory and congratulate the opposition on a "clean campaign." Like Irish wakes, the vigil often went on until dawn.

Modern television has changed all this. The national networks now begin coverage of election returns before the polls close and continue until the result is known—a result that is not usually long in coming. At one time poll workers carefully counted paper ballots, inscribed the results on official sheets and transported the ballot box to the county seat where officials would finally give the results to the media. Today, paper ballots are rare outside rural areas, and voting machines eliminate time-consuming ballot counting. Once the polls have closed, election officials simply read the results off the back of a machine that counts each vote as it is cast. Nor do the media wait for the results to be officially reported. They hire precinct watchers to read the results at the same time election officials do and report them to the networks over special telephone lines.[3] As a result the television networks can flash results on the screen moments after the polls have closed.

Television not only reports results that have been tabulated; it also "projects" winners on the basis of a very few returns. The procedure is the same one long used by politicians in a less extensive and less scientific way. "Key" precincts, those whose returns usually closely parallel the complete returns for the state in question, are identified beforehand and information about them is fed into computers. When returns from these precincts come in, the computer compares them with the returns of other years from the same precinct and projects who the eventual winner in the state will be. If the information originally stored in the computer was incomplete or inaccurate, the predictions will, of course, be wrong; but, so far, the networks have a commendable record for accuracy. As a result, the modern viewer often "knows" who has carried a state 30 minutes after the polls have closed, even though less than 5 percent of the vote may have been tabulated.

Very close elections cannot be called so quickly, and most of the network mistakes have come when the outcome was too hastily projected. On the whole, however, the projections have been accurate. There is no more "waiting for the downstate returns"; the computer has already taken such factors into account. In 1964, one network proclaimed Johnson the winner over Goldwater at 9:04 P.M., only a few hours after the first polls had closed. The 1968

---

[3]The television networks and the wire services have now pooled their efforts in creating a National Election Service to report election results.

and 1976 elections were much closer and were not projected until the morning after the election.

There has been criticism of television for projecting winners so swiftly, not only for spoiling election night parties but for actually influencing voters. With a three-hour time difference between East and West coasts, the networks have sometimes declared a winner based on East Coast returns while people were still going to the polls elsewhere. Many have claimed that this might influence the outcome of a close election by discouraging people from voting when they thought their candidate had already lost. A Senate committee held hearings on the subject but dropped the matter when several studies showed that network projections had little or no effect.[4]

In addition to reporting the results and projecting winners, the television networks also analyze the results and explain what has happened in demographic, social, and economic terms. Scholars have done this for years, of course, but not on election night. Computers are used to describe how the ethnic neighborhoods voted in Chicago, how a candidate is doing in farm areas, etc. The meaning of the election will be studied for years, but television, as usual, reports it first. In short, the viewer now knows as much about the outcome of the election before retiring on election night as it once took weeks to find out.

THE FINAL STAGES

When the final election results are in, the entire country knows who the next president and vice-president will be, but the outcome must still be formalized. In December, the electors who were chosen in November mark their ballots and mail them to Washington. When the Congress convenes in January, the ballots are opened before a joint session of the two houses and the official results announced. In nearly every American presidential election, this is a formality only. The election winner is already being referred to as the president-elect and has been preparing for weeks to assume office.

Presidential transitions are not easy for either the person leav-

---

[4]MacNeil, *The People Machine,* pp. 121–122.

ing office or the person coming into it. A "lame duck" president must carry on with presidential duties even though he carries less weight than before the election in domestic, political, and international circles. It is considered bad form for the president-elect to offer policy advice during the transitional period; an outgoing president does not usually seek it. The atmosphere of suspended animation that characterizes a presidential transition would probably cause some problems if a severe crisis should arise. For example, what should be the attitude of a president-elect should a nuclear confrontation with a foreign power develop in December? No one knows the answer because the country has been spared any such development, but the general attitude of presidents-elect has been that the country has only one president at a time, that the powers of the presidency do not come in stages but all at once. Today, an ordinary citizen; tomorrow, the most important elected official in the world.

At noon on January 20 following a presidential election, the term of the preceding president ends and that of the incoming president begins.[5] At a formal inauguration ceremony, the Chief Justice of the U.S. Supreme Court[6] swears in the president and the vice-president before members of Congress, government dignitaries, representatives of foreign governments, and a host of important well-wishers. The new chief executive makes an inauguration speech and a parade usually follows. A new president has begun the duties of office and a new presidential election process has begun.

---

[5]Before the adoption in 1933 of the Twentieth Amendment, presidents were inaugurated on March 4.
[6]In an emergency, a president may take the oath of office before any official authorized to administer oaths, even a notary public. After the assassination of President John F. Kennedy in 1963, Lyndon Johnson was sworn in as president by Federal Judge Sarah Hughes in the presidential plane at the Dallas airport.

AFTERWORD

This book has been written to explain the presidential nomination and election process. Its rationale is the value of individual participation at any stage in the process. And yet some have tended to ask, "Why bother? Can I make a difference?"

Yes, you can. "Now more than ever," to borrow a slogan coined by a former presidential contender, because the method by which a president is chosen is a screening mechanism over which you—the voter—can exert some real control.

The long and arduous process of "choosing the president" puts the presidential hopefuls up for scrutiny by giving you an opportunity to evaluate their performance: As *leaders*—their ability to inspire trust; as *administrators*—their organizational skills; and as *individuals*—their degree of honesty, competence, sensitivity, and integrity.

Their campaign organizations may be viewed as mini-White Houses—precursors of an administration-to-be. If you look closely you can see how they operate as money-managers, how realistic their proposals are, how they deal with the press, and how much personal contact they try to develop with the public.

And you can do more than just watch . . .

The thing to do is start asking questions—find out who and where the party leaders are. Call them, volunteer your services, ask about times and places of meetings, ask your neighbors about what's what politically in your area, call the League of Women Voters. The only qualification necessary for political involvement is interest.

No presidential election has ever been, or is likely to be, decided by one vote, but it is a statistical cliché that more than once a shift of relatively few votes in the right states would have changed the outcome under the electoral college system. The most drastic case in recent years was the 1960 election—when Nixon lost the presidential election by an average of only one vote per precinct.

The closer the balance between the parties in a state, the more important is the single vote, and now that we are beginning to have a real two-party system throughout the country, the competition for each vote is growing in practically every state. Even if the outcome is almost a foregone conclusion, a vote cast in a losing cause is not a wasted vote. It can be politically worthwhile as a way to build or retain strength for the future. If, for instance, every southern Republican had stopped voting during the years of Democratic domination of the South, the modern Republican party could never have developed as it has in recent years.

The legitimacy of the chief executive's leadership is affected by who elects the president to begin with. And if only a small fraction of the public turns out to vote the individual into office, our democratic system will fall short of its potential for people to vocalize their power. Changes in all aspects of our political system—some of which have been described in this book—mean that in 1980 American government rests far more than ever before in our history on individual participation, on *your* participation, at every stage in the election process.

APPENDIXES

Appendix A

PROVISIONS IN THE U.S. CONSTITUTION RELATING TO THE PRESIDENCY

UNITED STATES CONSTITUTION

ARTICLE II—THE PRESIDENT

Section 1. The executive Power shall be vested in a President of the United States of America. He shall hold his Office during the Term of four Years, and, together with the Vice-President, chosen for the same Term, be elected as follows.

Each state shall appoint, in such Manner as the Legislature thereof may direct, a Number of Electors, equal to the whole Number of Senators and Representatives to which the State may be entitled in the Congress: but no Senator or Representative, or Person holding an Office of Trust or Profit under the United States, shall be appointed an Elector.

The Congress may determine the Time of choosing the Electors, and the Day on which they shall give their Votes; which Day shall be the same throughout the United States.

AMENDMENT XII—PRESIDENTIAL ELECTORS

The Electors shall meet in their respective states and vote by ballot for President and Vice-President, one of whom, at least, shall not be an inhabitant of the same state with themselves; they shall name in their ballots the person voted for as President, and in distinct ballots the person voted for as Vice-President, and they shall make distinct lists of all persons voted for as President, and of all persons voted for as Vice-President, and of the number of votes for each, which lists they shall sign and certify, and transmit sealed to the seat of the government of the United States, directed to the President of the Senate;—The President of the Senate shall, in presence of the Senate and House of Representatives, open all the certificates and the votes shall then be counted;—The person having the greatest number of votes for President, shall be the President, if such number be a majority of the whole number of Electors appointed; and if no person have such majority, then from the persons having the highest numbers not exceeding three on the list of those voted for as President, the House of Representatives shall choose immediately, by ballot, the President. But in choosing the President, the votes shall be taken by states, the representation from each state having one vote; a quorum for this purpose shall consist of a member or members from two-thirds of the states, and a majority of all the states shall be necessary to a choice. And if the House of Representatives shall not choose a President whenever the right of choice shall devolve upon them, before the fourth day of March[1] next following, then the Vice-President shall act as President, as in the case of the death or other constitutional disability of the President.[2]—The person having the greatest number of votes as Vice-President, shall be the Vice-President, if such number be a majority of the whole number of Electors appointed, and if no person have a majority, then from the two highest numbers on the list, the Senate shall choose the Vice-President; a quorum for the purpose shall consist of two-thirds of the whole number of Senators, and a majority of the whole number shall be necessary to a choice. But no person constitutionally ineligible to the office of President shall be eligible to that of Vice-President of the United States. [Ratified in 1804]

AMENDMENT XX—LAME DUCK AMENDMENT

Section 3. If, at the time fixed for the beginning of the term of the President, the President elect shall have died, the Vice-President elect shall become President. If a President shall not have been chosen before the time fixed for the beginning of his term, or if the President elect shall have failed to qualify, then the Vice-President elect shall act as President until a President shall have qualified; and the Congress may by law provide for the case wherein neither a President elect nor a Vice-President elect shall have qualified, declaring who shall then act as President, or the manner in which one who is to act shall be selected, and such person shall act accordingly until a President or Vice-President shall have qualified.

Section 4. The Congress may by law provide for the case of the death of

---

[1]By the Twentieth Amendment, adopted in 1933, the term of the president is to begin on January 20.
[2]Under the Twentieth Amendment, Section 3, in case a president is not chosen before the time fixed for the beginning of his term, the vice-president elect shall act as president until a president shall have qualified.

any of the persons from whom the House of Representatives may choose a President whenever the right of choice shall have devolved upon them, and for the case of the death of any of the persons from whom the Senate may choose a Vice-President whenever the right of choice shall have devolved upon them. [Ratified in 1933]

D.C. AMENDMENT
(sent to states for ratification in August 1979)

Section 1: For the purposes of representation in Congress, election of the President and Vice-President, and article V of the Constitution, the District constituting the seat of government of the United States shall be treated as though it were a State.

Section 2: The exercise of the rights and powers conferred under this article shall be by the people of the District constituting the seat of government, and as shall be provided by the Congress.

Section 3: The twenty-third article of amendment to the Constitution of the United States is hereby repealed.

Section 4: This article shall be inoperative, unless it shall have been ratified as an amendment to the Constitution by the legislatures of three-fourths of the several States within seven years from the date of its submission.

Appendix B

THE PRESIDENTIAL OFFICE

Qualifications for office

- Natural-born citizen; at least 35 years old; 14 years or more a resident within the United States.

U.S. CONSTITUTION, ARTICLE II: *Section 1.* "No person except a natural-born citizen, or a citizen of the United States, at the time of the adoption of this Constitution, shall be eligible to the office of President; neither shall any person be eligible to that office who shall not have attained to the age of thirty-five years, and been fourteen years a resident within the United States."

AMENDMENT XII. "The electors shall meet in their respective states and vote by ballot for President and Vice-President, one of whom, at least, shall not be an inhabitant of the same state with themselves."

Term of office

- Four years, beginning on January 20 of the year following election.

U.S. CONSTITUTION, AMENDMENT XX: *Section 1.* "The terms of the President and Vice-President shall end at noon on the 20th day of January, and the terms of Senators and Representatives at noon on the 3rd day of January, of the years in which such terms would have ended if this article had not been ratified; and the terms of their successors shall then begin."

- No more than two terms or ten years.

U.S. CONSTITUTION, AMENDMENT XII. "No person shall be elected to the office of the President more than twice, and no person who has held the office of President, or acted as President, for more than two years of a term to which some other person was elected President shall be elected to the office of the President more than once. But this Article shall not apply to any person holding the office of President when this Article was proposed by the Congress, and shall not prevent any person who may be holding the office of President, or acting as President, during the term within which this Article becomes operative from holding the office of President or acting as President during the remainder of such term." [Ratified in 1951]

Presidential oath of office

- U.S. CONSTITUTION, ARTICLE II: *Section 1.* "Before he enter on the execution of his office, he shall take the following oath or affirmation: 'I do solemnly swear (or affirm) that I will faithfully execute the office of President of the United States, and will to the best of my ability, preserve, protect and defend the Constitution of the United States.' "

Salary

- **President**

$200,000 a year salary, taxable;
$50,000 a year expense allowance, taxable, to assist in defraying expenses resulting from his official duties;
$100,000 a year, nontaxable, may be expended for travel expenses and official entertainment.

U.S. CONSTITUTION, ARTICLE II: *Section 1.* "The President shall, at stated times, receive for his services, a compensation, which shall neither be increased nor diminished during the period for which he shall have been elected, and he shall not receive within that period any other emolument from the United States, or any of them."

- **Ex-President**

$66,000 a year lifetime pension, free mailing privileges, free office space;
Up to $90,000 a year for office help;
Secret Service protection for life;
$20,000 a year for widow.

- **Vice-President**

$79,000 a year salary, taxable;

$10,000 a year, taxable, for expenses;
Use of official residence.

Duties and powers of the president

U.S. CONSTITUTION, ARTICLE II: *Section 2.* (1) "The President shall be commander in chief of the army and navy of the United States, and of the militia of the several States, when called into the actual service of the United States; he may require the opinion, in writing, of the principal officer in each of the executive departments, upon any subject relating to the duties of their respective offices, and he shall have power to grant reprieves and pardons for offenses against the United States, except in cases of impeachment."

Section 2. (2) "He shall have power, by and with the advice and consent of the Senate, to make treaties, provided two thirds of the Senators present concur; and he shall nominate, and by and with the advice and consent of the Senate, shall appoint ambassadors, other public ministers and consuls, judges of the Supreme Court, and all other officers of the United States, whose appointments are not herein otherwise provided for, and which shall be established by law: but the Congress may by law vest the appointment of such inferior officers, as they think proper, in the President alone, in the courts of law, or in the heads of departments."

Section 3. "He shall from time to time give to the Congress information of the state of the Union, and recommend to their consideration such measures as he shall judge necessary and expedient; he may, on extraordinary occasions, convene both Houses, or either of them, and in case of disagreement between them, with respect to the time of adjournment, he may adjourn them to such time as he shall think proper; he shall receive ambassadors and other public ministers; he shall take care that the laws be faithfully executed, and shall commission all the officers of the United States."

Section 4. "The President, Vice-President, and all civil officers of the United States, shall be removed from office on impeachment for, and conviction of, treason, bribery, or other high crimes and misdemeanors."

Succession to the presidency

U.S. CONSTITUTION, AMENDMENT XXV: *Section 1.* "In case of the removal of the President from office or of his death or resignation, the Vice-President shall become President."

Section 2. "Whenever there is a vacancy in the office of the Vice-President, the President shall nominate a Vice-President who shall take office upon confirmation by a majority vote of both houses of Congress."

Section 3. "Whenever the President transmits to the President pro tempore of the Senate and the Speaker of the House of Representatives his written declaration that he is unable to discharge the powers and duties of his office, and until he transmits to them a written declaration to the contrary, such powers and duties shall be discharged by the Vice-President as Acting President."

Section 4. "Whenever the Vice-President and a majority of either the principal officers of the executive departments or of such other body as Congress may by law provide, transmit to the President pro tempore of the Senate and the Speaker of the House of Representatives their written declaration that the President is unable to discharge the powers and duties of his office, the Vice-President shall immediately assume the powers and duties of the office as Acting President.

"Thereafter, when the President transmits to the President pro tempore of the Senate and the Speaker of the House of Representatives his written declaration that no inability exists, he shall resume the powers and duties of his office unless the Vice-President and a majority of either the principal officers of the executive department or of such other body as Congress may by law provide, transmit within four days to the President pro tempore of the Senate and the Speaker of the House of Representatives their written declaration that the President is unable to discharge the powers and duties of his office. Thereupon Congress shall decide the issue, assembling within forty-eight hours for that purpose if not in session. If the Congress, within twenty-one days after receipt of the latter written declaration, or, if Congress is not in session, within twenty-one days after Congress is required to assemble, determines by two-thirds vote of both houses that the President is unable to discharge the powers and duties of his office, the Vice-President shall continue to discharge the same as Acting President; otherwise, the President shall resume the powers and duties of his office." [Ratified in 1967]

President	DIED IN	Vice-President AND WAS SUCCEEDED BY
W. H. Harrison	1841	John Tyler
Zachary Taylor	1850	Millard Fillmore
Abraham Lincoln	1865	Andrew Johnson
James A. Garfield	1881	Chester A. Arthur
William McKinley	1901	Theodore Roosevelt
Warren G. Harding	1923	Calvin Coolidge
Franklin D. Roosevelt	1945	Harry S Truman
John F. Kennedy	1963	Lyndon B. Johnson
	RESIGNED IN	
Richard M. Nixon	1974	Gerald R. Ford

Presidential succession has never yet gone beyond the vice-presidency. By the Presidential Succession Act of 1947 as amended, the line of succession to the presidency, first to last, is:

Vice-President
Speaker of the House
President pro tempore of
    the Senate
Secretary of State
Secretary of the Treasury
Secretary of Defense
Attorney General
Secretary of the Interior
Secretary of Agriculture
Secretary of Commerce
Secretary of Labor
Secretary of Health and
    Human Services
Secretary of Housing and
    Urban Development
Secretary of Transportation
Secretary of Energy
Secretary of Education

Vacancies in the vice-presidency

The office of the vice-president has been vacant 18 times, for a total of over 37 years.

Nine vice-presidents left vacant the office they were elected to serve in when they went to the White House to fill a presidential vacancy.

Seven vice-presidents died in office:

Vice-President	DIED IN	under President
George Clinton	1812	James Madison—1st term
Elbridge Gerry	1814	James Madison—2nd term
William R. King	1853	Franklin Pierce
Henry Wilson	1875	Ulysses S. Grant
Thomas A. Hendricks	1885	Grover Cleveland
Garret A. Hobart	1899	William McKinley
James S. Sherman	1912	William H. Taft

Two vice-presidents resigned: John C. Calhoun resigned in 1832 as vice-president under Andrew Jackson to become a U.S. senator. He had been vice-president since 1825—under both Jackson and John Quincy Adams. Spiro Agnew resigned in 1973 as vice-president under Nixon shortly before pleading "no contest" to charges of income tax evasion.

Appendix C

PRESIDENTIAL SUCCESSION—ARE CHANGES NEEDED?

One ripple effect of Watergate was citizens' startled discovery in 1974 that a president and a vice-president do not have to be elected, that under the Twenty-fifth Amendment they can be appointed by a president and confirmed by a majority vote of both houses of Congress. Thus, Richard Nixon appointed Gerald Ford as vice-president after Spiro Agnew's resignation. Gerald Ford succeeded to the presidency when Nixon resigned under the cloud of impeachment; and Ford appointed Nelson Rockefeller as vice-president.

This extraordinary sequence of events has prompted a reassessment of the Twenty-fifth Amendment, serious discussion of alternatives for presidential succession, and a fresh look at the office of vice-president.

The Constitution initially gave Congress the authority to provide by law for presidential succession. Congress implemented this responsibility under three successive laws that set forth the line of succession to the vice-presidency when the vice-president succeeds to the presidency:

- 1792 Act—President pro tempore of the Senate, Speaker of the House;
- 1886 Act—members of the cabinet in order of the establishment of their departments: State, Treasury, etc.;
- 1947 Act—Speaker of the House, President pro tempore of the Senate, members of the cabinet.

The primary purpose of the Twenty-fifth Amendment, ratified in 1967, was to provide for succession in case of presidential disability, a matter of concern ever since the assassination of Garfield and the illnesses of several presidents, a matter of greater urgency when Kennedy was assassinated. Sections 3 and 4 of the amendment provide in detail for declaring a president disabled and removing him temporarily or permanently from office.

Another purpose of the amendment was to clarify and confirm that "in case of the removal of the President from office or of his death or resignation, the Vice-President shall become President" rather than acting president. The Constitution had left this point ambiguous and open to various interpretations. When John Tyler succeeded to the presidency on the death of William Henry Harrison, he set a precedent by insisting on taking the oath of office as president rather than serving as acting president.

The ironic fact is that the first time the amendment was used, in 1973, it was in a set of circumstances considered little if at all at the time of ratification. Indeed, it is doubtful that the drafters and supporters of the amendment ever gave much thought to the consequences of Section 2: "Whenever there is a vacancy in the office of the Vice-President, the President shall nominate a Vice-President who shall take office upon confirmation by a majority vote of both houses of Congress." It is this section that is currently the subject of controversy and of proposals for repeal or modification.

The most vehement opposition to the Twenty-fifth Amendment comes from those who object in principle to a nonelected president and vice-president because they consider such a situation undemocratic and contrary to the intent of the Constitution. Those who are satisfied with the way the amendment worked in 1973 and 1974 point out that the presidential and vice-presidential appointees were subjected to such close scrutiny by Congress that more was known about them—certainly in the case of the vice-president—than if they had gone through the usual nomination and election procedures. They also point out that the re-signations of Agnew and Nixon were unprecedented and too bizarre to serve as the model for a new constitutional amendment.

Proposals for changing the Twenty-fifth Amendment range from outright repeal to minor tinkering and include special elections under a variety of circumstances, return to the succession Act of 1947, or selection of a president and/or a vice-president by the electoral college.

The idea of special elections is not new; the first succession act, in effect for almost 100 years, provided for special elections, and bills have been introduced since to implement this idea. Those who favor special elections (including Sens. John Pastore, Edward Kennedy, and William D. Hathaway) point to the final phrase of Clause 6, "or a President shall be elected," as constitutional support for this procedure. The Twenty-fifth Amendment does not preclude this possibility.

One of the more seriously considered proposals is to hold a special election when an appointed vice-president succeeds to the presidency with more than one year left in the term. Under this system, there would be no chance that a president and vice-president might come from different parties. Other alternatives (suggested by Sen. Howard H. Baker, Jr. and Reps. Patsy T. Mink and Joshua Eilberg) are that the electoral college should select a new vice-president when the vice-president becomes president under the Twenty-fifth Amendment, or select both president and vice-president if both offices are vacant.

Appendix D

CONSTITUTIONAL AMENDMENTS EXPANDING THE SUFFRAGE

AMENDMENT XV: *Section 1.* "The right of citizens of the United States to vote shall not be denied or abridged by the United States or by any State on account of race, color, or previous condition of servitude." [Ratified in 1870]

AMENDMENT XVII: *Section 1.* "The Senate of the United States shall be composed of two Senators from each State, elected by the people thereof, for six years; and each Senator shall have one vote. The electors in each State shall have the qualifications requisite for electors of the most numerous branch of the State Legislatures." [Ratified in 1913]

AMENDMENT XIX: *Section 1.* "The right of citizens of the United States to vote shall not be denied or abridged by the United States or by any State on account of sex." [Ratified in 1920]

AMENDMENT XXIII: *Section 1.* The District constituting the seat of Government of the United States shall appoint in such manner as the Congress may direct:

A number of electors of President and Vice-President equal to the whole number of Senators and Representatives in Congress to which the District would be entitled if it were a State, but in no event more than the least populous State; they shall be in addition to those appointed by the States, but they shall be considered, for the purposes of the election of President and Vice-President, to be electors appointed by a State; and they shall meet in the District and perform such duties as provided by the twelfth article of amendment. [Ratified in 1961]

AMENDMENT XXIV: *Section 1.* "The right of citizens of the United States to vote in any primary or other election for President or Vice-President, for electors for President or Vice-President, or for Senator or Representative in Congress, shall not be denied or abridged by the United States or any State by reason of failure to pay any poll tax or other tax." [Ratified in 1964]

AMENDMENT XXVI: *Section 1.* "The right of citizens of the United States, who are eighteen years of age or older, to vote shall not be denied or abridged by the United States or by any State on account of age." [Ratified in 1971]

Appendix E

EVOLUTION OF THE PRESIDENTIAL NOMINATION PROCESS

1789–1792	Early nonpartisan system. Washington twice elected unanimously with no formal nomination.
1796	Beginning of party control of political nominations generally and legislative caucus method of making presidential nominations. John Adams is last Federalist to be elected.
1800–1820	Federalist and Democratic-Republican (Jeffersonian) nominees, chosen in legislative caucus, battle regularly in elections.
1820–1824	"Era of Good Feeling." Monroe renominated by Democratic-Republicans by common consent with no formal action and wins in electoral college 231–1.
1824	Jackson defies legislative caucus and wins nomination of Tennessee legislature. Fails in election when presidential choice thrown into House of Representatives and John Quincy Adams wins in "corrupt bargain."
1828	Jackson is again nominated by Tennessee legislature and wins election, signaling new era by gaining power as result of well-organized popular movement. Caucus method of nomination now in disrepute.
1831	First national party convention in modern sense held in

Baltimore by Anti-Masonic party. William Wirt nominated but party fails to survive long.

1832 First Democratic national convention held in May in Baltimore as Jacksonian revolution continues. Jackson (for president) and Van Buren (for vice-president) nominated and elected.

1839 With convention method of nomination now becoming established, Whigs hold their first national convention. They elect two presidents but cannot survive the slavery turmoil.

1856 First Republican national convention held in June in Philadelphia as new major party emerges. Fremont is first presidential candidate.

1860 Republicans nominate first winning presidential candidate in Abraham Lincoln.

1860–1908 Democratic and Republican national conventions dominate presidential nominations except for brief threat from Populists in 1890s.

1910 Oregon passes first presidential primary law as charges of bossism in conventions grow. Other states follow.

1912 First presidential election year with presidential primaries. New method allows Theodore Roosevelt to demonstrate popular support, but Taft wins nomination.

1972 Reforms in the Republican and Democratic parties.

1976 Thirty-one states held primaries.

1980 Thirty-five states holding primaries.

Appendix F

1980 ELECTORAL VOTES BY STATE

Total: 538   Needed to elect: 270

State	Electoral Vote	State	Electoral Vote
California	45	Connecticut	8
New York	41	Colorado	7
Pennsylvania	27	Kansas	7
Illinois	26	Mississippi	7
Texas	26	West Virginia	6
Ohio	25	Arkansas	6
Michigan	21	Arizona	6
New Jersey	17	Oregon	6
Florida	17	Nebraska	5
Massachusetts	14	Maine	4
North Carolina	13	New Hampshire	4
Indiana	13	Rhode Island	4
Virginia	12	South Dakota	4
Georgia	12	Montana	4
Missouri	12	Idaho	4
Wisconsin	11	Utah	4
Tennessee	10	New Mexico	4
Maryland	10	Hawaii	4
Louisiana	10	Alaska	3
Minnesota	10	Nevada	3
Alabama	9	Wyoming	3
Washington	9	North Dakota	3
Kentucky	9	Vermont	3
South Carolina	8	Delaware	3
Iowa	8	District of Columbia	3
Oklahoma	8		

Appendix G

PROTECTION OF CANDIDATES FOR THE PRESIDENCY

The assassination of President William McKinley in 1901 provided the impetus for initiating Secret Service protection of presidents. But presidential aspirants were not given this security option until the assassination of Senator Robert Kennedy 67 years later. After that shocking event, President Lyndon Johnson issued an executive order calling for protection of all announced major candidates for the presidency. This later became law, with the provision that candidates could decline protection. In the 1976 campaign more than half a dozen candidates requested and received Secret Service protection.

A five-person advisory committee determines whether prospective candidates meet the criteria for protection. To qualify, a candidate must:
- be a declared candidate;
- have received financial contributions and be likely to qualify for federal matching funds; and
- conduct an active campaign.

There are, however, exceptions to these criteria. In 1979 Senator Edward Kennedy was given Secret Service protection even though he had not formally declared his candidacy for president.

Appendix H

SIGNIFICANT PRESIDENTIAL ELECTIONS

With the electoral college system it is possible for a candidate to be elected by a majority of the electoral votes, even though he may not have had a majority of the popular votes throughout the nation (majority means one more than half).

Elected without popular majorities, but with popular pluralities (the most votes) in a field of more than two candidates:[1]

James K. Polk in 1844	James A. Garfield in 1880	Woodrow Wilson in 1916
Zachary Taylor in 1848	Grover Cleveland in 1884	Harry S Truman in 1948
James Buchanan in 1856	Grover Cleveland in 1892	John F. Kennedy in 1960
Abraham Lincoln in 1860	Woodrow Wilson in 1912	Richard M. Nixon in 1968

---

[1]Examples of third-party presidential nominees in this century who have received electoral votes: in 1912 Theodore Roosevelt, The Progressive (Bull Moose) party—88 electoral votes; in 1924 Robert M. La Follette, Sr., Progressive—13 electoral votes; in 1948 J. Strom Thurmond, States' Rights party (Dixiecrat)—39 electoral votes; in 1968 George C. Wallace, American Independent party—46 electoral votes.

Elected with neither majorities nor pluralities of popular votes:

John Quincy Adams in 1824 (election decided by House of Representatives)

Rutherford B. Hayes in 1876 (election decided by congressional electoral commission)

Benjamin Harrison in 1888

The closest presidential election in 76 years. In 1960 Kennedy's official plurality after recounts was 118,263 votes in a record 68 million plus. A total of 224,931 voters did not mark their ballots for president. His plurality percentage was by the thinnest margin—less than one half of 1 percent. The electoral votes were 303 for Kennedy; 219 for Nixon; 15 for Senator Harry F. Byrd of Virginia (from electors in Mississippi, Alabama, and Oklahoma). Kennedy won seven states by less than 1 percent of the popular vote in each. These seven states had a total of 77 electoral votes—much more than enough to swing the election to him. (Delaware, Hawaii, Illinois, Minnesota, Missouri, New Jersey, New Mexico.) Five additional states gave Kennedy all their electoral votes (87) with a less than 2 percent plurality of popular vote. (Michigan, Nevada, Pennsylvania, South Carolina, Texas.) Altogether these 12 states with a less than 2 percent popular plurality have a total electoral vote of 164, far more than half the electoral votes Kennedy received to win the election.

All-time electoral vote record. Since 1900 only three Democratic presidents, Franklin D. Roosevelt, Lyndon Johnson, and Jimmy Carter have received an absolute majority of the popular vote. In 1936 Roosevelt reached an all-time record of 98.5 percent of the electoral vote with a substantial 59 percent of the popular vote. Johnson in 1964 won 90 percent of the electoral vote with 61 percent of the popular vote.

BIBLIOGRAPHY

Adamany, David W., and George E. Agree. *Political Money—A Strategy for Campaign Financing in America.* Baltimore: Johns Hopkins University Press, 1975.

Alexander, Herbert E. "Communications and Politics: The Media and the Message." *Law and Contemporary Problems.* Duke University School of Law, Durham, N.C., Spring 1971.

———. *Political Finance: Reform and Reality.* Philadelphia: American Academy of Political and Social Science, 1976.

Bach, Stanley, and George T. Sulzner. *Perspectives on the Presidency: A Collection.* Lexington, Mass.: D. C. Heath, 1974.

Barber, James D., ed. *Choosing the President.* Englewood Cliffs, N.J.: Prentice-Hall, 1974.

Blackman, Paul H. *Presidential Primaries and the 1976 Elections.* Washington, D.C.: Heritage Foundation, 1975.

Blevens, Leon W. *The Young Voters Manual.* Totawa, N.J.: Littlefield, 1973.

Bode, Ken. "Black Democrats at the Tower of Babel." *New Republic,* December 27, 1975.

———. "Polls and Pols." *New Republic,* January 17, 1976.

Bone, Hugh. *American Politics and the Party System.* 4th ed. New York: McGraw-Hill, 1971.

Bruno, Jerry. *The Advance Man.* New York: Bantam Books, 1971.

Campbell, Angus, et al. *The American Voter.* New York: John Wiley & Sons, 1960.

Cantor, Robert D. *Voting Behavior and Presidential Elections.* Itasca, Ill.: F. E. Peacock, 1975.

Casey, Carol F. *Procedures for Selection of Delegates to the Democratic and Republican 1980 National Conventions: A Preliminary Survey of Applicable State Laws and Party Rules.* Congressional Research Service, Library of Congress, October 1979.

Chester, Edward W. *Radio, Television and American Politics.* New York: Sheed & Ward, 1969.

Civil Rights Commission. *Voting Rights Act—10 Years After.* Washington, D.C.: Government Printing Office, 1975.

Colburn, Kenneth S., and George A. Dalley. "The Congressional Black Caucus and Joint Center for Political Studies Guide to Participation in the Delegate Selection Process for the Democratic and Republican Party Conventions in 1976." Washington, D.C.: Third National Institute for Black Elected Officials, 1975.

Crouse, Timothy. *The Boys on the Bus: Riding with the Campaign Press Corps.* New York: Ballantine Books, 1974.

Current History. "American Political Reform" issue, August 1974.

Democratic National Committee, Washington, D.C.
   The Call for the 1976 Democratic National Convention. 1975.
   Delegate Selection Rules for the 1976 Democratic National Convention, 1975.
   Democrats All. Report of the Commission on Delegate Selection and Party Structure, 1973.
   Mandate for Reform. Report of the Commission on Party Structure and Delegate Selection, 1970.

DeVries, Walter, and V. Lance Tarrance. *Ticket Splitter: A New Force in American Politics.* Grand Rapids, Mich.: William B. Eeerdmans, 1972.

Diamond, Robert, ed. *Presidential Elections Since 1789.* Washington, D.C.: Congressional Quarterly, Inc., 1975.

Drew, Elizabeth. "Running." *New Yorker,* December 1, 1975.

Dunn, Delmer D. *Financing Presidential Campaigns.* Washington, D.C.: Brookings Institution, 1972.

Factual Campaign Information. Compiled under the direction of the Secretary of the Senate. Washington, D.C.: Government Printing Office, March 1976.

Flanigan, William H. *Political Behavior of the American Electorate.* Boston: Allyn & Bacon, 1968.

Gorman, Joseph. *Elections: Electoral College Reform.* Washington, D.C.: Congressional Research Service, Library of Congress, January 1976.

————. *Elections: Presidential Primaries.* Washington, D.C.: Congressional Research Service, Library of Congress, issue brief, continuously revised.

Hadley, Arthur T. *The Invisible Primary.* Englewood Cliffs, N.J.: Prentice-Hall, 1976.

Hadley, Charles D. "The Nationalization of American Politics: Congress, the Supreme Court and the National Political Parties." Unpublished manuscript. University of New Orleans, Department of Political Science, November 1975.

Hess, Stephen. *The Presidential Campaign: The Leadership Selection Process After Watergate.* Washington, D.C.: Brookings Institution, 1974.

Hiebert, Ray E., Robert F. Jones, John d'Arc Lorenze and Ernest A. Lotito, eds. *The Political Image Merchants: Strategies for the Seventies.* Washington, D.C.: Acropolis Books, 1975.

Hofstadter, Richard. *American Political Tradition.* New York: Random House, 1948.

Hoopes, Roy. "The Press and the Campaigns: Back on the Bus in '76." *Democratic Review,* October/November 1975.

Humphrey, Hubert H. "How the President Can Help Improve Vice-Presidential Selection." *Congressional Record,* Vol. 119, No. 202, December 21, 1973.

Johnson, Walter. *How We Drafted Adlai Stevenson.* New York: Alfred A. Knopf, 1955.

Keech, William, and Donald Matthews. *The Party's Choice.* Washington, D.C.: Brookings Institution, 1976.

Kerr, Virginia. "The ABCs of Delegate Selection." *Ms.,* January 1976.

Key, V. O., Jr. *Politics, Parties and Pressure Groups.* 5th ed. New York: Thomas Y. Crowell, 1964.

Lang, Kurt, and Gladys Engel Lang. *Voting and Non-Voting: Implications of Broadcasting Returns Before Polls Are Closed.* Waltham, Mass.: Blaisdell, 1968.

League of Women Voters Education Fund. *Election '76: Issues Not Images.* Washington, D.C., 1976.

League of Women Voters of the United States. *Who Should Elect the President?* Washington, D.C., 1969.

MacNeil, Robert. *The People Machine: The Influence of Television on American Politics.* New York: Harper & Row, 1968.

Malbin, Michael. "Political Report/Democratic Delegate Rules Influencing Candidates' Strategies." *National Journal,* December 6, 1975.

———. "Political Report/New Campaign Finance Law Faces Legal, Political Tests." *National Journal,* July 12, 1975.

———. "Political Report/Party System Approaching Crossroads in 1976 Election." *National Journal,* May 31, 1975.

Matthews, Donald. *Perspectives on Presidential Selection.* Washington, D.C.: Brookings Institution, 1973.

May, Ernest R., and Janet Fraser. *Campaign, '72.* Cambridge, Mass.: Harvard University Press, 1973.

Mazmanian, Daniel A. *Third Parties in Presidential Elections: Studies in Presidential Selection.* Washington, D.C.: Brookings Institution, 1974.

McGinniss, Joe. *The Selling of the President 1968.* New York: Trident, 1969.

Minow, Newton N., John B. Martin, and Lee M. Mitchell. *Presidential Television.* Twentieth Century Fund Report. New York: Basic Books, 1973.

Movement for a New Congress. *Vote Power.* Englewood Cliffs, N.J.: Prentice-Hall, 1970.

Nomination and Election of the President and Vice President of the

United States. Compiled under the direction of the Secretary of the Senate. Washington, D.C.: Government Printing Office, March 1976.

Parris, Judith N. *The Convention Problem: Issues in Reform of Presidential Nominating Procedures.* Washington, D.C.: Brookings Institution, 1972.

Parris, Judith N., and Richard Baine. *Convention Decisions and Voting Records.* Washington, D.C.: Brookings Institution, 1973.

Perry, James M. *The New Politics: The Expanding Technology of Political Manipulation.* New York: Clarkson N. Potter, 1968.

————. *Us and Them: How the Press Covered the 1972 Elections.* New York: Clarkson N. Potter, 1972.

Phillips, Kevin P. *The Emerging Republican Majority.* Garden City, N.Y.: Doubleday, 1970.

————. *Mediacracy: American Parties and Politics in the Communications Age.* Garden City, N.Y.: Doubleday, 1975.

Polsby, Nelson W., and Aaron Wildavsky. *Presidential Elections: Strategies of American Electoral Politics.* 4th ed. New York: Charles Scribner's Sons, 1976.

Pomper, Gerald. *Voters' Choice: Varieties of American Electoral Behavior.* New York: Harper & Row, 1975.

Ranney, Austin. *Curing the Mischiefs of Faction: Party Reform in America.* Berkeley, Calif.: University of California Press, 1975.

Reeves, Richard. *A Ford, Not a Lincoln: The Decline of American Leadership.* New York: Harcourt Brace Jovanovich, 1975.

Republican National Committee. *Report of the Rule 29 Committee.* Washington, D.C., 1975.

Ripon Society and Clifford W. Brown, Jr. *Jaws of Victory.* Boston: Little, Brown, 1974.

Roper, Burns W. "Distorting the Voice of the People." *Columbia Journalism Review,* November/December 1975.

Scammon, Richard M. *America Votes,* vol. 10. Washington, D.C.: Congressional Quarterly, Inc., 1973.

Scammon, Richard M., and Ben J. Wattenberg. *The Real Majority.* New York: Coward-McCann, 1971.

Schwartzman, Edward. *Campaign Craftsmanship: A Professional Guide to Campaigning for Elective Office.* New York: Universe Books, 1973.

Senior Power: A Political Action Handbook for Senior Citizens. Washington, D.C.: United Steel Workers of America with the Cooperation of Kramer Associates, 1974.

Shadegg, Stephen C. *How to Win an Election.* New York: Taplinger, 1964.

Strouse, James C., and Howard Rosenstock. "Television and Political Malaise: The 1972 Election with a Longitudinal Perspective . . . or The Medium is NOT the Massage." Unpublished manuscript. University of Maryland, College Park, Md., November 1975.

Sundquist, James L. *Dynamics of the Party System: Alignment and*

Realignment of Political Parties in the United States. Washington, D.C.: Brookings Institution, 1973.

Thompson, Hunter S. *Fear and Loathing: On the Campaign Trail '72.* New York: Popular Library, 1973.

White, Theodore H. *The Making of the President 1972.* New York: Atheneum, 1973.

———. *The Making of the President 1968.* New York: Atheneum, 1969.

———. *The Making of the President 1964.* New York: Atheneum, 1965.

———. *The Making of the President 1960.* New York: Atheneum, 1961.

Wyckoff, Gene. *The Image Candidates: American Politics in the Age of Television.* New York: Macmillan, 1968.